# HEALTHY
# DOG

## The Ultimate Fitness Guide
## for You and Your Dog

### Health Experts
### Share Their Secrets

**By Arden Moore**

D1309114

**BOWTIE**
**P R E S S**®

A Division of BowTie, Inc.
Irvine, California

Karla Austin, Business Operations Manager
Ruth Strother, Editor-At-Large
Erin Kuechenmeister, Production Editor
Rebekah Bryant, Editorial Assistant

Nick Clemente, Special Consultant
Jen Dorsey, Associate Editor
Michelle Martinez, Assistant Editor
Bocu & Bocu, Book Design

**Library of Congress Cataloging-in-Publication Data**
Moore, Arden.
  Healthy dog : the ultimate fitness guide for you and your dog / by
Arden Moore.
    p. cm.
  ISBN 1-889540-91-9 (soft cover with flaps : alk. paper)
  1. Dogs. 2. Dogs—Health. 3. Dogs—Exercise. I. Title.
SF427.M735 2004
636.7'0893--dc21

                            2003013332

Bowtie Press®
A Division of BowTie, Inc.
3 Burroughs
Irvine, California 92618

Printed and Bound in Singapore
10 9 8 7 6 5 4 3 2 1

✦ ✦ ✦ ✦ ✦ ✦ ✦ ✦ ✦

# ACKNOWLEDGMENT

✦ ✦ ✦ ✦ ✦ ✦ ✦ ✦ ✦

*I wish to thank all the medical doctors, veterinarians, nutritionists,*
*dog trainers, fitness instructors, and other professionals who generously*
*shared their expertise to make this book truly fit for people and dogs.*
*Special thanks to Dan Hamner, M.D.; Christine Zink, D.V.M., Ph.D.;*
*Lowell Ackerman, D.V.M.; Dale L. Anderson, M.D.; Lyn Huffaker, D.V.M., Ph.D.;*
*Selene Yeager; Liz Palika; Joely Johnson; and Annie Glasgow. Finally,*
*a big thanks to Flo Frum for her photographic talents.*

★　★　★　★　★　★　★　★　★

*To Jazz, my energetic corgi, and to all those who see the value
of teaming up with their dogs to stay in shape*

# CONTENTS

# FOREWORD

As a sports medicine physiatrist in New York City, I've long valued the magic of movement. As I tell my patients, purposeful movement serves as a healing tool to help the body self-repair and self-renew. With each stretch and stride we can revitalize and recharge our bodies and our minds. Regular physical activity tones muscles and releases biochemicals that boost mental concentration and elevate moods. When you're fit, you feel and look good—inside and out.

Exercise promotes a natural high. I'm living proof. At age 62 I regularly run marathons (occasionally setting age group records), and I often bypass the elevator to walk up the 10 flights to my apartment. What keeps me on track? I'm blessed to have not one but two motivating workout partners: Rae Baymiller, my girlfriend; and Zook, my spirited four-year-old Japanese chin. Rae, age 59, became the oldest woman to complete the Chicago Marathon in under 3 hours, with a time of 2 hours and 55 minutes for the 26.2-mile course. We love traveling to different parts of the country to compete in road races and marathons. We encourage one another.

Zook doesn't run marathons, but he's definitely a four-legged sprinter. He loves to zoom back and forth along the length of our 42-foot wooden deck for an aerobic workout. He regularly joins us for casual jogs through Central Park. At the end of the jog, we walk the five blocks back home with Zook happily setting the pace. And sometimes he has the energy to climb up the flights of stairs. When he begins to pant and linger on a step, I know that's my cue to hoist him into my arms and carry him up the rest of the way. I regard him as my furry 15-pound free weight as we scale the stairs.

I also recognize the second key component to staying fit: nutrition. Rae and I fill our plates with healthy foods. We also watch what goes into Zook's food bowl. He gets fed high-quality commercial dog food twice a day. The only "people" food he eats is a multivitamin-packed cereal and occasionally tiny pieces of broiled, lean fish or turkey. The result? All three of us are limber and at healthy weights. We

sleep soundly and wake up energized for a full day of activities.

Over the years I've authored medical papers, magazine articles, and books on human fitness. But this is the first time I've been asked to write a foreword for a dog book. I chuckled at first when my friend Arden Moore asked me. Then I paused and realized that Arden offers a refreshingly new approach to fitness: the ultimate cross-training, cross-species guide that helps both you and your dog stay in shape.

Arden reveals an often-overlooked secret weapon to combating couch potato syndrome and potato chip consumption: the pet dog. Our canine chums prove day after day that exercise can be doggone fun. Each chapter in her book is loaded with terrific tips designed to assist you and your dog to achieve—and maintain—good health.

View today as the first day of the rest of your life. Forget past excuses as to why you skipped your gym workout or bypassed the bike ride. Recognize how fortunate you are to share your life with a tail-wagging pal. Look into his smiling eyes, join him in a full-body wiggle, and then engage in exercise. Indoors or out. Or both.

Give your dog the gift of health—and let him do the same for you.

— Dan Hamner, M.D.

Physiatrist, sports medicine expert, author, and visiting professor of rehabilitation and medicine at the New York Hospital-Cornell Medical Center in New York City. And a lifelong dog lover.

☆ ☆ ☆ ☆ ☆ ☆ ☆ ☆ ☆

# INTRODUCTION

☆ ☆ ☆ ☆ ☆ ☆ ☆ ☆

Is sharing a pepperoni pizza your idea of spending quality time with your dog? Or is it lounging together on the couch for a night of must-see TV? Have your walks around the neighborhood turned into mutual strides to the refrigerator? One in three Americans is overweight—that's old news. The more startling news is that, according to the American Veterinary Medical Association, nearly one in two adult dogs is plump. Our canine chums are following us down the path to obesity, all the way to the last table scrap!

Fortunately, we can fight the fat war and have fun in the process. The solution is simple: team up with your ever-loyal workout partner—your dog. Together, the two of you can become fit and healthy.

This book blends the world of pets and health to create a unique cross-species, cross-training approach to life. In each chapter you'll read on-target advice and tips from leading medical doctors, veterinarians, nutritionists, dog trainers, and fitness instructors who enthusiastically team up to empower you and your tail wagger with helpful food and fitness tips.

This book also spotlights people and their dogs who have conquered the battle of the bulge. Be inspired by Maureen Keller, who shed a few dress sizes thanks to a Labrador retriever named Bunky. Learn how Stephanie Huber keeps her arms toned without the use of free weights and in the process gets plenty of friendly licks from Alfred, her Yorkshire terrier. And feel your hips swivel with the tale of Elvis, a 12-year-old Labrador who displays puppy-like energy with his owner, Ganay Johnson.

My current partner is Jazz, a young Pembroke Welsh corgi who motivates me to walk, hike, toss a ball, and put the "play" back in my day. And at mealtimes, we chow down on great food that fills us up, not out. I certainly don't need a personal trainer, gym membership, or expensive in-home equipment with Jazz around. As a regular contributor to *Dog Fancy* and *Prevention* magazines, I value the special friendship that dogs give us as well as the importance of making healthy choices. I care about what I eat and what I feed Jazz. And when it comes to a motion motivator, Jazz is the leader of the pack. So, call your dog by your side and read this book in good health—for the both of you.

Paws up!

—Arden

# CHAPTER 1

✶ ✶ ✶ ✶ ✶ ✶ ✶ ✶ ✶ ✶

# WHY THE BATHROOM SCALES DON'T LIE

✶ ✶ ✶ ✶ ✶ ✶ ✶ ✶ ✶ ✶

I t's easy to blame the drier for the sudden shrinkage of your clothes. As for your dog, it's easy to buy her a larger collar because you rationalize that she is growing normally.

A few years ago when I was 25 pounds heavier, I convinced myself that my bathroom scale was off-kilter. I would weigh myself and mentally subtract 5 or 10 pounds from where the arrow landed. It had to be the scale's fault; I certainly didn't weigh that much. I would also snip off the size tags on my clothes. But I was only fooling myself.

There's no magic weight-loss wand one can wave that—poof!—melts pounds and replaces a slow-moving waddle with an energetic stride. Yet. But,

each of us possesses the power to permanently zap excess pounds. Achieving fitness is the best gift we can give to ourselves and to our canine companions. The payoffs are priceless:

- a better fit for clothes and collars
- fewer visits to the doctor and the veterinary clinic, saving both money and time
- the ability to walk, run, twist, bend, and reach without a lot of huffing and puffing
- the feeling of waking up refreshed, not achy
- the ability to concentrate and learn new skills (and for your dog, new tricks)
- the feeling of being more mentally alert and energetic
- a closer friendship with your dog
- added years to your life and life to your years

## Obesity Dangers

Your dog isn't opening up the refrigerator on her own and helping herself to midnight snacks. Often, the culprit behind a chubby dog is her owner. Dogs can easily become overweight or obese, and owners often have a hard time recognizing this because the gain can be gradual. Or some people may innocently think it's cute when their corgis look like hairy waddling ottomans. Owners may not realize the impact a few extra pounds can have; gaining 1 or 2 pounds may not sound like much, but for a 10-pound dog it is equivalent to a person gaining more than 25 pounds. More importantly, leading veterinary nutritionists say excess weight can reduce the length of a dog's life by as much as 20 percent.

A combination of too much food (especially table scraps) and too little exercise can lead to the development of severe chronic conditions such as diabetes, high blood pressure, heart problems, arthritis, muscular injuries, and respiratory problems in dogs. In addition, excess pounds can increase the risk for certain cancers to develop. Sound familiar? The health risks for canines mirror many of our own. And, as with us, hereditary and breed factors also play roles.

In both people and dogs, obesity is one of the leading health problems. According to several sources, including the American Medical Association and the USDA, there is a difference between obesity and being overweight. Obesity occurs when a person (or dog) weighs 30 percent or more above the ideal weight for her age, gender, and bone size (or a particular dog breed). Overweight is defined as being between 20 and 25 percent above the ideal weight among peers.

## Rely on the Rib Test

Is your dog flabby or fit? To judge, you need to look at your dog's body condition instead of a scale. Do this at-home test:

- **Stand in front of your dog.** Exam her standing body profile. She should have a clearly defined abdomen, slightly tucked up behind her rib cage.
- **Stand over your dog.** Most dogs, when standing, have an hourglass shape so you should be able to see your dog's waist.
- **Gently run your fingers over your dog's backbone and spread your hands across her rib cage.** You should be able to feel each rib.

In an obese dog, fat deposits are readily visible on the neck, limbs, base of tail, and spine. There is also a noticeable absence of the tucked-in waist or abdomen. In an overweight dog, the waist is barely visible and you can see fat deposits over the lumbar area and base of the tail. You can feel the ribs, but just barely. In a fit dog, you can feel the ribs; there is not a lot of fat covering them. Looking from the side, you can see the abdomen tucked up and you will see the hourglass shape when you look at your dog from above. A dog who's too thin has protruding and highly visible ribs, pelvic bones, and lumbar vertebrae.

## Where Do You Fit In?

It is equally important for people to understand what constitutes a healthy weight. For example, don't let the bathroom scale be the sole source of determining whether you are losing weight. Muscle weighs more than fat, so better indicators are if you drop inches and clothing sizes, not pounds. Here are some ways to determine a desirable body weight for you, according to the National Institutes of Health:

**Women:** 100 pounds of body weight for the first 5 feet of height, 5 pounds for each additional inch

**Men:** 106 pounds of body weight for the first 5 feet of height, 6 pounds for each additional inch

Add 10 percent for a large frame size; subtract 10 percent for a small frame size. If you are unsure of your frame size, consult your physician.

These results will help you calculate your daily calorie requirements. Here are some guidelines for adults, as provided by the American Academy of Sports Dietitians and Nutritionists.

**Very physically active:** 18 calories per pound of desirable body weight

**Normal activity level:** 15 calories per pound of desirable body weight

### Breeds Prone to Obesity

basset hounds
beagles
cairn terriers
cocker spaniels
collies
dachshunds
Doberman pinschers
Labrador retrievers
Scottish terriers
shelties
West Highland terriers

*A good way to determine successful weight loss is to chart inches lost around the waist and arms.*

**Light activity level or age 55 or over:** 13 calories per pound of desirable body weight

**Sedentary or overweight:** 10 calories per pound of desirable body weight

Let's illustrate with a 40-year-old woman who is 5 ft 4 in. tall with a medium body frame and normal activity level. Her ideal weight is 125 pounds, or 100 + (5 × 5) = 125 and her daily calorie needs to maintain this weight is 1,875, or 125 × 15 = 1,875. A 60-year-old man who is 6 ft tall with a medium frame should weigh about 178 pounds, or 106 + (6 × 12) = 178. He will maintain his weight if he doesn't exceed 2,314 calories a day, or 178 × 13 = 2,314.

Of course, these examples represent baselines. Use them strictly as a guide. You also need to find out what your fat-to-muscle ratio is because muscle weighs more than fat and burns more calories. Two common methods of determining fat-to-muscle ratio include the skin-fold test and bioelectrical impedance. In the first method, your fat percentage is determined by the amount of fat between the pincers of a skin-fold caliper. For the second, you step on a bioelectrical impedance device, which safely sends electrical impulses through your body to identify how much fat and muscle tissue you have. The skin-fold caliper is available at local drugstores and fitness centers. The bioelectrical impedance device is available through most physicians or medical clinics.

You can find out the areas of your body that need trimming by using a sewing tape measure. Wrap the tape around your upper arm, chest, waist, hips, thighs, and calves. Write down the amount of inches at each of these sites and the date. Consult your physician to identify healthy measurements for your body type. Use this as your starting point and remeasure after you've been in a fitness program for eight weeks.

Having a good idea of your target weight and daily calorie needs, you need to determine your fitness level before beginning any exercise program. My friend, Selene Yeager of Emmaus, Pennsylvania, is a certified personal trainer, tri-athlete, fitness consultant, and author of *Selene Yeager's Perfectly Fit: 8 Weeks to a Sleek and Sexy Body* (Rodale, 2001). She shares her home with her equally athletic husband, Dave Pryor, and their terrific Labrador mixes named Annabelle and Sonja. Yeager invites you to try these easy tests to gauge your overall fitness:

*Try the toe-touch test to gauge your flexibility.*

## The Flamingo Stand

This exercise rates your sense of balance. Stand on one leg and keep your knee slightly bent. Raise your other leg so that your knee is bent like a flamingo's. Keep your arms at your sides and close your eyes.

| Time (in seconds) | Rating |
| --- | --- |
| Under 10 | Poor |
| 10–20 | Fair |
| 20–30 | Good |
| 30 or more | Excellent |

## The Toe-Touch Test

This exercise tests your flexibility. Stand with your feet a shoulder-width apart. As you keep your legs straight, bend forward from your waist. Your goal is to touch the floor with your fingers.

| Reach | Rating |
| --- | --- |
| Above your ankles | Poor |
| Your ankles | Fair |
| Your toes | Good |
| Fingertips on floor | Great |
| Palms flat on floor | Superb |

## The Stairs Test

This exercise tests your aerobic fitness level. Find a flight of stairs with 30–40 steps. Walk or run up and down the stairs several times. If necessary, hold the handrail. Wait 60 seconds and then take your pulse for 10 seconds (place two fingers on the side of your neck). Multiply that number of beats by 6.

| Pulse | Rating |
| --- | --- |
| Under 90 | Excellent |
| 90–100 | Good |
| 101–120 | Fair |
| Above 121 | Poor |

## The Push-Up Test

This exercise tests your upper body strength. Get into a push-up position with your legs bent so that your hands and knees support your weight. Keep your back straight as you lower your chest to 3 inches above the floor. Push back up—that's one push-up. Want to gauge your fitness? Use the handy chart below. The goal is to perform push-ups with the performance ratings based on your age. For example, if you're 20 and can do only 20 push-ups, you have some work to do. In contrast, if you're 40 and can do 24 or more push-ups, then you've earned an excellent rating.

| Age | Push-ups | Rating |
| --- | --- | --- |
| 20–29 | Under 22 | Poor |
| | 23–29 | Fair |
| | 30–35 | Good |
| | 36 plus | Excellent |
| 30–39 | Under 18 | Poor |
| | 19–23 | Fair |
| | 24–30 | Good |
| | 31 plus | Excellent |
| 40–49 | Under 12 | Poor |
| | 13–17 | Fair |
| | 18–23 | Good |
| | 24 plus | Excellent |
| 50–59 | Under 11 | Poor |
| | 12–16 | Fair |
| | 17–20 | Good |
| | 21 plus | Excellent |
| 60 plus | Under 4 | Poor |
| | 5–11 | Fair |
| | 12–14 | Good |
| | 15 plus | Excellent |

*The stairs test is an easy way to test your aerobic fitness level.*

*Work with your veterinarian and doctor to create the ultimate fitness plan for you and your canine friend.*

## Book a Date with Your Doctor

Once you've declared war on flab, congratulate yourself on taking an empowering first step. Then grab the phone and make two calls: one to your doctor and one to your dog's veterinarian. Never begin a weight loss or exercise program for you or your dog without consulting your physician and your dog's veterinarian.

The pre-exercise physical exams for you and your dog are nearly identical. You both have to get up on an exam table (fortunately, the people table is usually not an icy-cold stainless steel version). A medical professional checks the heart, lungs, muscular and skeletal conditions as well as the eyes, ears, and mouth. Both of you will be given a head-to-toe (or head to tip of the tail) examination to evaluate your overall health.

Go prepared with a list of questions and answers to potential questions from you doctor. Know your eating habits, activity habits, and any medications you or your dog are taking. Be prepared to inform the doctor about any changes in eating or elimination habits. Have your or your dog had any recent injuries? Surgeries? Medical conditions?

The not-so-secret way to fitness is to eat less and exercise more. Don't be lured by quick-loss pitches. Resist crash diets for you and your dog. A dog that is 30 percent overweight should take about six months to reach an ideal weight through reduced food portions. This slow but steady plan takes off the pounds safely—and keeps them off. People should aim to lose 1 to 2 pounds a week.

Play it smart and heed your doctor's advice. Use this opportunity to work with medical experts who can assist you in establishing a healthy game plan that best suits you and your dog's age, activity level, and health status. Bring a notebook and jot down any advice that your doctor or veterinarian gives you. Don't rely on your memory once you leave the clinic. If you and your dog have been diagnosed as being overweight, it's not the end of the world. It's the beginning of a better, new you!

---

### Success Story: Maureen Keller and Bunky

Maureen Keller needed a workout partner to help her shed the 25 pounds she gained after ending a long relationship. Looking for a fresh start, she relocated from the Philadelphia area to Denver. She knew she would feel self-conscious at the local fitness club, filled with thin spandex-clad exercisers. "A size 12 was too tight, but I refused to buy a size 14," says Keller, 52, a university media relations director.

That's when she eyed her perfect exercise mate: Bunky, her sister's Labrador retriever who had a wide girth from too much couch lounging. The pair panted in harmony after their first brisk round-the-block walk. But slowly and steadily, they increased their distance until they could complete a two-and-a-half-hour walk in stride along a scenic canal. By summer's end, Keller was back into a size 8 and filled with a renewed sense of accomplishment. Bunky, age eight, had lost 10 pounds off his 85-pound frame and regained puppy-like energy. "I couldn't have accomplished this without my best workout buddy, Bunky," says Keller.

# CHAPTER 2

* * * * * * * * *

# BONE UP ON YOUR NUTRITION KNOWLEDGE

* * * * * * * * *

The nutritional needs of humans and canines are basically the same. Whether man, woman, shih tzu or Saint Bernard, six key nutrients come into play in any healthy diet: carbohydrates, fats, proteins, vitamins, minerals, and water.

These nutrients are responsible for the growth, maintenance, and repair of our bodies. Carbohydrates, fats, and protein provide the major ingredients for building tissue and producing energy in the body. Vitamins, minerals, and water perform other roles such as maintaining a healthy red blood cell supply, keeping bones strong and dense, and keeping tissues hydrated and body temperatures regulated. How much of each nutrient we require differs, based on our individual needs. Let's take a closer look at each nutrient.

## Give Me a C for Carbohydrates

Carbohydrates—sugars, starches, and fibers—serve as the body's top-notch source of energy. They are divided into two groups:

● **Simple carbohydrates:** Common types include

*Vegetables and rice are carbohydrates.*

*Cereal can be a good source of fiber.*

table sugar (sucrose); honey; natural sugars found in fruit, vegetables, and milk; and fructose (found in many soft drinks). Corn, oatmeal, and rice are also simple carbohydrates. These types of carbohydrates consist of small molecules that are rapidly absorbed in the body.

● **Complex carbohydrates:** Also called starches, complex carbs are found in fruits, vegetables, pastas, breads, and grain foods. They are larger molecules than simple carbs, so the body needs more time to break them down; this causes them to reach the bloodstream more slowly than do simple carbohydrates. Some kinds of foods, such as vegetables, fall in both the simple and complex carbohydrate categories because some individual foods may be either simple or complex.

## Facts on Fiber

Fiber is a friend to you and all Fidos. An indigestible carbohydrate, it cruises through the digestive system without being absorbed by the body, but it plays many major roles. Fiber aids the passage of food through the digestive system and helps form firm stools. Dietary fiber also provides a feeling of full-

*The "good fat" found in products like olive and soybean oil can lower cholesterol.*

ness. Too little fiber in a diet can cause diarrhea; too much fiber can create constipation. Either extreme can lead to dehydration.

Eating fiber in the right amount can help keep you and your dog at a healthy weight; you feel fuller on fewer calories. It can also protect you both from colon cancer, and lower your cholesterol (to reduce your risk for heart disease). Good fiber sources are apples, baked potatoes, bananas, green beans, broccoli, high-fiber cereals, and any dog's favorite: peanut butter.

## Good Fat, Bad Fat

One key fact: not all fat is bad.

Dietary fat provides a good, concentrated source of energy, maintains healthy skin (and a dog's glossy coat), improves the taste of foods, aids in digestion, and transports fat-soluble vitamins A, D, E, and K to the intestines for proper absorption. A dog with an adequate supply of dietary fat has healthy skin and footpads and is less likely to develop allergies. Fat also helps our bodies use carbohydrates and proteins more efficiently. In fact, compared to carbohydrates and protein, fats contain about two and a half times more energy per pound.

The key to healthy fat intake? You guessed it—moderation. Also, focus on sources of "good" fats—foods containing monounsaturated fat and polyunsaturated fat. These good fats, found in oils such as olive oil, soybean oil, safflower oil, and corn oil, may help reduce the risk of chronic diseases such as heart disease, stroke, and cancer; and they lower cholesterol levels.

Sidestep "bad" fats—foods high in saturated fats—that can contribute to heart disease, strokes, and high cholesterol levels. We know these bad fats all too well. They come disguised in many of our favorite foods such as French fries, cheeseburgers, and thick milk shakes.

## The Power of Protein

Proteins act like construction workers in the body—they repair the body's infrastructure. Protein is derived from animals and plants such as beef, chicken, pork, soybeans, corn, and wheat, and it repairs tissue and produces tendons, cartilage, nails, and hair. Protein also provides energy, ensures muscle growth, and aids blood, hormones, and the body's immune system. Remember this number: 23. That's the number of

*Eggs are a good source of protein for those who don't eat meat.*

*Humans, unlike dogs, cannot produce their own vitamin C and must get it from other sources.*

## The Vitality of Vitamins

The primary purpose of vitamins is to promote and regulate various physiological processes in the body. They help convert calories to energy and create blood cells. Generally, people and dogs cannot produce vitamins. One notable exception: unlike us, dogs can produce their own vitamin C from glucose. Humans need to get vitamin C from oranges or other fruits.

Vitamins are divided into two groups: fat-soluble (A, D, E, and K), and water-soluble (thiamine, riboflavin, niacin, pantothenic acid, folic acid, vitamin $B_6$, choline, biotin, vitamin C, and vitamin $B_{12}$). More details on these vitamins and their importance can be found in Chapter 4: The Inside Scoop on Supplements and Vitamins.

## Must-Have Minerals

Minerals are inorganic nutrients that are not produced in either the human or canine body, but are needed for normal body function. They contribute to the strength of teeth and bones and assist in numerous enzymatic functions. Minerals are divided into two groups: major (or macro) and trace minerals. For people and dogs, there should be a delicate balance between the amounts of the different major and trace minerals. Major minerals particularly vital

essential and nonessential amino acids—the building blocks of protein—that are absorbed by our bodies. For your canine pal, the 10 key amino acids are arginine, histidine, isoleucine, leucine, lysine, methionine, phenylalanine, threonine, tryptophan, and valine.

*The calcium found in milk is the most abundant mineral in the body.*

to dogs—and people—include calcium, phosphorus, magnesium, and sulfur. Important trace minerals include iron, iodine, zinc, selenium, copper, manganese, and cobalt.

For both people and dogs, the most abundant major mineral—hands down—is calcium.

## Water—Drink Up!

Your life—and your dog's—depends on drinking adequate amounts of clean water. Water not only

*Both humans and dogs need plenty of water each day.*

quenches thirst but it also helps regulate body temperature, keeps tissues lubricated, aids in food digestion, and flushes toxins and waste matter from the body. And, here's a strange-but-true tidbit: the amount of water found in a human and a canine body is identical—70 percent.

When people work up a sweat, the skin pores open and perspiration pours out. That's the body's internal air-conditioning system kicking in to help it avoid heat exhaustion. Dogs are not so fortunate. Lacking head-to-toe sweat glands, they can sweat only through their footpads. Because of this, dogs are at a greater risk of dehydration when they exert energy in hot weather. If your dog's water bowl is licked dry, he cannot grab a water bottle from the refrigerator, twist open the cap, and gulp away his thirst. Dogs depend on us to provide them with fresh drinkable water. So whenever you reach for a glass of water, also check the water level in your dog's bowl. It's a good habit to maintain.

## Digest This

Most people have great confidence in the power of nutrition. In fact, 74 percent of Americans agree that food and nutrition play a strong role in maintaining or improving overall health,

*Human and dogs should chew and swallow slowly for optimum digestion.*

and 93 percent believe that certain foods provide some medicinal healing benefits, according to a 2001 national study by the International Food Information Council. (You can read more about the study at www.ific.org.) But when we bite, chew, and swallow food, we rarely give much thought to what happens to it once it heads down that long tunnel called the esophagus. The path is the same for person or dog: the chewed food heads to the stomach and breaks down.

The human and canine digestive systems operate much like factory assembly lines: when everything is humming along, bites of food and sips of drink travel down the esophagus into a series of organs, each of which has a specific task to fulfill. Along the way, ingested food is splashed with different secretions and broken down into small molecules that can be easily absorbed. The body's digestive system churns, converting food into fuel. On cue, the circulatory system enters the scene and, acting as the body's shipping agent, dispatches these fortifying nutrients throughout the body.

In the simplest terms, digestion depends on two processes: mechanical (chewing and swallowing) and enzymatic (secretion and absorption). It also requires clear communication among the different body systems. The stomach, for example, may alert the small intestine with the message, "Hey, I just received a big shipment of food from the esophagus, so be prepared." And the small intestine may respond to the stomach by saying, "Pace yourself. I need to catch up with what you sent me an hour ago."

## Key players in both human and canine digestion

✔ **Mouth:** Here, bites of food are chewed and lubricated with saliva. The salivary glands produce an enzyme that starts to break down carbohydrates into smaller molecules.

✔ **Esophagus:** Think of this long narrow tube as an elevator that sends food down from the mouth and into the stomach. In a healthy person, the elevator button is always in the down position. It features a ring-like valve at its bottom that opens and allows food to enter the stomach.

✔ **Stomach:** Most of the digestive action occurs here. Hardworking enzymes, digestive juices, and smooth stomach muscles go to work on the newly arrived food, reducing it to liquid form. Chemical digestion of proteins begins here.

✔ **Liver:** This vital organ produces a digestive juice called bile, which is essential for the digestion and absorption of fats. The bile acids dissolve the fat into the watery contents of the intestines. In between meals, bile is stored in the gallbladder.

✔ **Pancreas:** Another crucial organ, this one provides digestive enzymes to the small intestine to help digest fats and carbohydrates.

✔ **Small intestine:** This is the last stop for chemical digestion and the place where almost all nutrients are absorbed.

✔ **Large intestine:** This area is responsible for three key jobs: absorption of water, fermentation of bacteria, and formation of feces.

## WHY IS DIGESTION IMPORTANT?

The bagel you had for breakfast or that slice of pizza you ate for lunch cannot be used as nourishment by your body in their original forms. The same applies to the kibble your dog wolfed down at his morning meal. Everything you and your dog eat and drink must be downsized into small molecules of nutrients that can be absorbed into the bloodstream and carried to cells from your head to your toes—or in your dog's case to the tip of his tail.

## WHAT CONTRIBUTES TO DIGESTIVE PROBLEMS?

Many factors can cause one's digestive system to perform less than perfectly. Eating habits, age, certain medications, and stress all influence how well one's digestive system functions. Eating on the run can lead to indigestion and heartburn, and stress can reduce blood flow to the liver, which results in fewer nutrients being available for absorption by the body. Aspirin, antibiotics, and steroids sometimes cause imbalances to the digestive system. Finally, as we—and our dogs—get older, our appetites tend to decrease, our taste buds become impaired, and our stomachs secrete less hydrochloric acid, which is important for the proper digestion and absorption of ingested food.

## WHAT HORMONES CONTROL DIGESTION?

Just as a successful corporation relies on independent auditors to make sure financial solvency is maintained, the digestive system depends on three key hormones to control its functions: gastrin, secretin, and cholecystokinin (CCK). These hormones are unleashed into the blood of the digestive tract, pass through the heart and arteries, and return to the digestive system, where they activate digestive juices and get organs to perform their specific jobs.

Here's a closer look at these hormones and why they are critical to both people and dogs.

- **Gastrin:** This hormone instructs your stomach to make an acid capable of digesting and dissolving food particles. It also helps maintain the normal growth of the linings in your stomach, small intestine, and large intestine.

- **Secretin:** This hormone alerts your pancreas to dispatch a digestive juice loaded with bicarbonate. It also cues your stomach to produce pepsin (an enzyme that breaks down proteins) and tells your liver to produce bile (to digest fats).

- **Cholecystokinin (CCK):** This hormone causes your pancreas to make enzymes and prompts your gallbladder to empty itself.

## Weighing In—Calculating Calories

By definition, a calorie is a unit by which energy is measured. Food energy is measured in kilocalories (1000 calories equal 1 kilocalorie). As an example, 1 kilocalorie is the amount of energy needed to heat 1 gram (g) of water one degree centigrade. Diets for adults, on average, are based on consuming 2,000 calories per day. But the number of calories you need to maintain a healthy weight depends on your body composition, metabolism, and activity level. You may require more or fewer calories.

### HOW TO CALCULATE YOUR DAILY CALORIE NEEDS—A QUICK ESTIMATE

The following quick estimate of your calorie needs is exactly that. It doesn't allow for factors such as metabolic rate, age, or body fat percentage. It shouldn't be used as an exact calculation of calorie requirements; it's simply a ballpark calorie assessment.

### QUICK ESTIMATE OF CALORIE NEEDS

If you are moderately active, multiply your current weight in pounds by 15. If you are typically inactive, multiply your current weight in pounds by 13.

### EXAMPLE OF CALORIE NEEDS

You weigh 150 pounds and lead a relatively inactive life. Your daily caloric needs are 150 x 13 = 1,950 calories. This is the total number of calories your body needs in order to maintain its current weight.

## The Truth About Carnivores

Contrary to popular belief, canines are not carnivores (strictly meat eaters). They are omnivores, animals who feed on both animal and plant substances. True, your doggy's great-great-great-granddad may have hunted prey in the prairie but remember, his prey (rabbits and birds) were herbivores who ate only plants. Therefore, your dog's digestive system is engineered to digest and absorb protein from plant sources as well as from meat.

Dogs aren't strictly meat eaters.

Few dogs need to chow down 2,000 calories per day. Like humans, a dog's caloric requirements depend on his size, age, activity level, and health condition. But here is a general guideline to help you determine how many calories to feed your dog:

| DOG'S WEIGHT | DAILY CALORIC NEEDS |
| --- | --- |
| 10 pounds | 400 to 500 |
| 20 pounds | 700 to 800 |
| 40 pounds | 1,100 to 1,400 |
| 75 pounds | 1,750 to 2,000 |

No matter what you weigh, one thing remains constant: 1 pound of fat equals 3,500 calories. This applies to both you and your dog. To lose 1 pound, you need to burn 3,500 more calories than you eat—ideally over the period of one week.

## What's on a People Food Label?

The U.S. Food and Drug Administration (FDA) requires food manufacturers to provide consumers with information about certain nutrients. The next time you shop at the supermarket, pick up a pack-

*Read food labels to plan meals in appropriate portion sizes.*

aged food item and take a close look at the Nutrition Facts label. All labels are required to include information about the following boldfaced nutrients, and some labels include information about some or all of the other listed nutrients. Here are the nutrients listed in the order in which they must appear on human food labels (the rules for dog food are not as stringent):

**total calories**

**calories from fat**

calories from saturated fat

**total fat**

**saturated fat**

polyunsaturated fat

monounsaturated fat

**cholesterol**

**sodium**

potassium

**total carbohydrate**

**dietary fiber**

soluble fiber

insoluble fiber

**sugars**

sugar alcohol (such as sugar substitutes xylitol, mannitol and sorbitol)

**protein**

**vitamin A**

percent of vitamin A present as beta-carotene

other essential vitamins and minerals

**vitamin C**

**calcium**

**iron**

## UNDERSTANDING FOOD LABELS

The FDA requires Daily Values (DVs) to be listed on food packages. DVs have been established for the following energy-producing nutrients: fat, saturated fat, total carbohydrate (including fiber), and protein; and for cholesterol, sodium, and potassium, which do not contribute calories.

DVs are based on the number of calories consumed per day with a baseline of 2,000 for an adult and are calculated as follows:

- fat based on 30 percent of calories and less than 65 g
- saturated fat based on 10 percent of calories and less than 20 g
- carbohydrate based on 60 percent of calories and less than 300 milligrams (mg)
- protein based on 10 percent of calories
- fiber based on 11.5 g of fiber per 1,000 calories
- sodium not to exceed 2,400 mg

## NUTRIENT CONTENT CLAIMS

Terms such as free and light must meet certain standards set by the FDA. Here are the legal definitions:

**Free:** A product must contain no fat, saturated fat, cholesterol, sodium, sugars, or calories to earn this label. For example, calorie-free means the item contains fewer than 5 calories per serving, and sugar-free and fat-free both mean the item has less than .5 g per serving.

**Low:** The food can be eaten frequently without exceeding dietary guidelines for one or more of the following components: fat, saturated fat, cholesterol, sodium, or calories. So, low-fat would apply to foods containing 3 g or less of fat per serving and low-sodium foods would contain 140 mg or less per serving.

**Light:** A food product contains one-third fewer calories or half the fat of the referenced food.

**Healthy:** A healthy food must be low in fat and saturated fat and contain limited amounts of cholesterol and sodium.

**Reduced or less fat:** The food contains at least 25 percent less fat per serving than the regular version.

## UNDERSTANDING YOUR NUTRITIONAL NEEDS

The FDA's established Daily Value for total fat, saturated fat, total carbohydrate, dietary fiber, and protein is based on a 2,000-calorie reference diet for an adult. But maintaining a healthy weight requires more than simply eating 2,000 or fewer calories per day. What you eat and in what amounts also play key roles.

*A balanced diet is the key to good health for both humans and dogs.*

Aim for this breakdown of percentages of essential nutrients:

**Total Fat:** 30 percent of total calorie intake

**Saturated Fat:** 10 percent of total calorie intake

**Total Carbohydrates:** 60 percent of total calorie intake

**Protein:** 10 percent of total calorie intake. In addition, strive for dietary fiber intake of 11.5 grams per 1,000 calories.

## Deciphering Dog Food Labels

Many of us are paying greater attention to the food labels found on our pet's food containers. Unfortunately, dog food labels can be confusing because they are not required to list all ingredients or percentages of caloric and fat intake.

The Association of American Feed Control Officials (AAFCO) established that all quality commercial dog food products should contain the following:

- guaranteed analysis of nutrients
- ingredient listing in descending order of predominance by weight
- additives listing
- net weight
- manufacturer contact information, including a toll-free consumer information number
- nutritional adequacy statement indicating if the product provides complete and balanced nutrition for all dogs or for a particular life stage
- feeding instructions that offer a general guideline
- caloric statement

*Veterinary nutritionists recommend that dog food contain at least 18 percent protein.*

As in human food, additives are added to commercial dog foods to enhance their quality, flavor, and appearance and to preserve freshness. Most commonly used additives include antioxidants (to keep fat from becoming rancid), antimicrobial agents (to slow down spoilage), colors (to improve appearance), and emulsifiers (to keep water and fat together).

Veterinary nutritionists recommend that commercial dog food for adult dogs contain no less than 18 percent protein. And even though your dog can get his protein needs from animal and plant origins, his complete source of protein comes from eating only animal-based foods such as lean meat, eggs, and whole milk.

## HOW TO READ A DOG FOOD LABEL

Commercial dog food labels should include the following information:

- **Product name:** The brand name and the specific food or formula contained in the can or bag must be stated in addition to the weight in grams and ounces.
- **Ingredient list:** Ingredients must be listed in descending order so that the most prevalent part of the diet is listed first, followed by each ingredient in order of weight.
- **Guaranteed analysis:** This lists the amounts of each ingredient contained in the food. For information on minimum nutrient guidelines established by the AAFCO, visit www.aafco.org.
- **Feeding instructions:** The label must indicate how much of the food to feed a dog per day.

The feeding instructions are broken down by weight of dog but should be considered a baseline. Your dog, depending on his activity level and other factors, may require more or less food.

- **Nutritional adequacy claim:** This section lists the life stage such as maintenance, for growth, or all life stages for which the food is made. AAFCO guidelines require the label to state whether the food provides complete and balanced nutrition for a particular life stage or is meant as a treat or a supplement.

### Success Story: Traci Bryant and Dudley

Dudley, as described by his owner, Traci Bryant, "is a beautiful, 80-pound chocolate Labrador with a high-energy level that's contagious."

Each morning, Bryant, of Germantown, Maryland, fills the blender with a variety of fruits and vegetables, hits the puree button, pours the liquid goodness into a glass, and gulps it down before heading for her three-mile run with Dudley. Dudley patiently taps his tail waiting for his nutritious pre-jog meal: a cup full of fresh bits of carrots, celery, grapes, oranges, apples, and whatever other fresh ingredients are available.

"This may be Dudley's favorite part of the day," says Bryant. "He comes running when he hears the juicer start and sits, wagging his tail and drooling, while we juice—it's pretty comical." Comical indeed, but the daily routine helps the pair work together to eat nutritious, energy-yielding foods. The payoff for both is that they maintain healthy weights and toned bodies.

# CHAPTER 3

✦ ✦ ✦ ✦ ✦ ✦ ✦ ✦ ✦ ✦

# EAT WELL WITHOUT BECOMING A CHOWHOUND

✦ ✦ ✦ ✦ ✦ ✦ ✦ ✦ ✦ ✦

The next time you stroll to the refrigerator or food pantry with your faithful chubby canine waddling close by, ask yourself this: what do I have to lose? As you sit down to eat a snack or drink a soda, WAIT and think about WEIGHT. Extra pounds are often the behind-the-scenes culprit that contribute to life-threatening diseases such as: diabetes, hypertension, heart problems, pain, and muscle weakness in both people and dogs. Being overloaded with unnecessary weight contributes to almost all orthopedic problems, especially pain and stiffness in the back and lower extremities.

Dale L. Anderson, M.D., a physician from St. Paul, Minnesota, offers this vivid description of the importance of maintaining a healthy weight: "You cannot drive a Mack truck on Volkswagen tires. Take it off. Take it off—the extra pounds. Tastefully, slowly, and sensibly."

The first bit of advice: delete the word *diet* from your vocabulary. I'll show you simple ways to alter your eating habits so that you can maintain a healthy weight so you'll never again have to step on the bathroom scale with trepidation. I'll also share savvy tips to keep your dog from becoming a plump pooch.

Be good to your digestive system by adopting these eating habits:

● **Book time for breakfast.** Opt for meals loaded with protein and fiber. After eight hours of sleep, your body needs fuel—energy—to get you going in the morning. Breakfast is a meal never to be missed.

*Make breakfast an essential part of each morning.*

- **Drink plenty of water.** Keep a water bottle near you at your desk and in your car, and have a glass of water at mealtimes to keep you hydrated. Plain $H_2O$ actually enhances the taste of food and fills you up so you don't eat as much.

- **Chew slowly.** The take-one-bite-and-swallow eating style can cause big chunks of food to lodge in your throat or slow down your digestive process. Chewing slowly helps your body digest the food and enables you to enjoy the meal more satisfactorily.

- **Salute your appetizer allies.** If you eat a healthy salad or drink a low-fat cup of soup before the main course, you will be able to cut down on your caloric intake. Eating warm meals with a delicious aroma can actually cut down on food consumption, too.

- **Relegate meats to side dish status.** Select a lean cut of beef or chicken and make sure it is never bigger than 3 ounces—about the size of a deck of playing cards. Make the main feature on your plate steamed broccoli or some other vegetable that is low in calories and high in nutritional value.

- **Take the dinner plate pace test.** During a meal, check the plates of your eating companions. If your plate is empty and their plates are still three-fourths full of food, that's a cue that you're eating too fast.

- **Wait twenty minutes before dishing up seconds.** Your digestive system takes about twenty minutes to communicate the feeling of fullness (satiety) to your brain. Drink a glass of water after your first helping and you may discover you aren't as hungry for that second helping as you thought.

- **Eat more broccoli and broiled fish.** Green vegetables are great sources of fiber and essential nutrients. Fish provides healthy omega fatty acids, which your body needs.

- **Avoid animal fats and vegetable, saturated, and trans-fatty oils.** Better choices are olive, walnut, and canola oils.

- **Turn off the TV.** Instead of wolfing down food while watching your favorite sitcom, try paying more attention to the food and engaging in friendly and calm conversation with your dinner mates.

- **If you're eating alone, read the paper.** Purposely turn the pages of the reading material with your fork-holding hand so you are forced to put the fork down and slow down your chewing. Or do a crossword puzzle or, even better, read the comic page.

- **Grab the leash and take your dog on a brisk 20- or 30-minute walk after—or before—dinner.** Your strides go a long way toward keeping your body toned and ready to digest your meal.

*A 30-minute walk each day benefits the entire family.*

- **Eat five small meals a day instead of three big ones.** Your body is able to digest smaller portions more easily than large meals because it does not have to deal with a big load of food at one time. Your body's digestive system performs better when it can pace itself with smaller, more frequent meals.
- **Forget what mom told you.** Never clean your plate, especially at a restaurant. Restaurant portions are often two to four times bigger than your daily dietary needs. To avoid overeating at restaurants, bring half of your meal home in a doggy bag and enjoy it the next day.
- **Get your just desserts.** Order low-calorie sorbet or fresh fruit instead of the fat-laden pecan pie à la mode or slice of double chocolate cake.

*Fresh fruit is a healthy dessert alternative.*

## Liquidate 'Waist-Full' Calories

You could gain up to 36 pounds in one year without taking a single bite, cautions Dr. Anderson. Fruit juices, soft drinks, whole milk, and coffee or tea loaded with cream and sugar are brimming with hidden calories. If you drink one 8-ounce glass of milk a day, you ingest the caloric equivalent of one "fat" pound each month. Triple that if you also drink one can of soda and one small glass of fruit juice each day. You risk gaining 3 pounds a month—or, a whopping 36 pounds in a single year!

### LIQUID CONSUMPTION ALERT

| | | |
|---|---|---|
| 4 ounces of juice | = | 100 to 120 calories |
| 8 ounces of milk | = | 100 to 150 calories |
| 12 ounces of soda | = | 120 calories |
| 12 ounces of beer | = | 100 to 130 calories |

If you were to drink the above liquids every day, your calorie consumption could top 3,500 in one month. And 3,500 calories equals 1 pound of fat.

# Go for Quantity and Quality

How would you like to eat all you want and still lose weight? It's possible! The key is food selection. Most adults who consume fewer than 2,000 calories a day can keep their weight steady. But frequent trips to fast-food restaurants can quickly exceed that 2,000-calorie limit.

Fill your plate with these low-calorie, low-fat choices:

| BREAKFAST | TOTAL CALORIES |
|---|---|
| Fruit cup with English muffin and jam | 200 |
| 2 raisin bread slices with low-sugar jam | 145 |
| 1 1/2 cups Frosted Flakes with non-fat milk | 240 |

| LUNCH | TOTAL CALORIES |
|---|---|
| A sandwich on pumpernickel bread with 2 ounces of smoked salmon, cucumbers, and capers | 235 |
| Bowl of minestrone soup | 110 |
| A sandwich on five-grain bread with veggie lunchmeat, lettuce, tomato and coleslaw | 240 |
| Veggie burger on sesame bun with tomato, onion pickle, catsup, and relish and 4 pretzel rods | 350 |

| DINNER | TOTAL CALORIES |
|---|---|
| 5 ounces shrimp, red bell peppers and onions with two portobello mushrooms, six asparagus spears, and corn on the cob | 290 |
| 3 ounces of broiled salmon, 1 cup steamed broccoli, an oven-browned potato, mixed salad with 1 tablespoon dressing, and 3 ounces of wine | 420 |
| 3-ounce grilled chicken breast, one medium baked sweet potato topped with 2 teaspoons brown sugar and 1 teaspoon margarine, 1 cup cooked spinach with lemon juice, and one whole wheat roll | 475 |

| SNACKS | TOTAL CALORIES |
|---|---|
| One low-calorie frozen fudge bar | 30 |
| 4 ounces frozen sorbet | 80 |
| Half of honeydew melon | 80 |
| 5 ounces grapes | 70 |
| Baked apple with raspberries | 100 |
| 1 cup trail mix | 160 |

## FORTIFYING FOODS

The real skinny on slimming down is selecting meals featuring these marquee headliners: whole grains, fruits, fish, lean meats, and green veggies. Please your palate and keep extra pounds at bay with these healthy choices:

- **Grab some whole grain bread.** Beyond its terrific taste, each slice of whole grain bread packs at least 3 g of dietary fiber. And fiber fills you up but doesn't fill you out because it does not contain fat.

- **Bring on the beans.** A half-cup of three-bean salad (kidney beans, lima beans, and black beans) averages from 6 to 8 g of fiber.

- **Go a little nutty.** Munch a handful of almonds or walnuts each day. Or sprinkle a salad with sunflower seeds. In moderation, nuts are a wonderful source of monounsaturated fats—a true heart protector.

- **Get hooked on fish.** Fresh or frozen fish is easily caught. So don't pass up a plate of broiled or poached salmon, tuna, perch, or cod—but skip the butter. These fish are swimming with omega-3 fatty acids, substances proven to elevate high-density lipoprotein (HDL), your "healthy" type of fat. An elevated HDL helps ward off arterial vascular disease. Fish oils also benefit joint function.

- **Be an advocate of avocados.** This fruit contains about 30 g of fat, but a few slices of avocado in a salad or sandwich once or twice a week offer you a tasty source of oleic acid, a monounsaturated fat.

- **Stick with strawberries.** These bright red gems contain high levels of antioxidants. In fact, strawberries are part of an all-star cast of antioxidants that work to neutralize free radicals, those nasty particles that damage cells and can lead to cancer.

- **Go bananas—and oranges.** These colorful fruits are loaded with potassium and vitamin C that not only lower blood pressure, but also stimulate an enzyme in your body that food researchers believe may help remove plaque from arterial walls.

- **Go for the green.** Spinach and kale—two dark leafy greens—feature plenty of vitamin C and vitamin K and act as antioxidants in fighting off cancer. And more good news: the 2000 Nurses' Health Study from Harvard reported that participants who ate spinach and kale regularly enjoyed up to 40 percent fewer cataract surgeries.

- **Crunch some carrots.** As Bugs Bunny would say, "What's up, doc?" The answer: carrots—along with their orange cousins squash and pumpkin—contain chemicals that inhibit tumor growth and fight cancer.

- **Strive for grape expectations.** Eating grapes, especially those with deeply colored skin, may protect you against heart disease and possibly prevent degenerative brain diseases such as Alzheimer's disease.

- **Find your blueberry thrill.** Why not consider these baby blues for dessert instead of a thick slab of banana cream pie? This versatile berry can be added to cereals, salads, pancakes, muffins, smoothies, yogurt, sauces, chutney, and dessert toppings. One cup of blueberries contains only 80 calories and 0 g of fat. During a USDA-sponsored study at the Human Nutrition Center on Aging at Tufts University, in North Grafton, Massachusetts, researchers discovered that among 40 fruits and vegetables, blueberries rank number 1 in antioxidant activity. Blueberries have been shown to improve balance, coordination, and memory.

- **Feast on "fake" foods.** Switch to using no-fat "fake" butter, cheese, sour cream, mayonnaise, and no-yolk egg substitutes or egg whites. Fat-free hot dogs and fat-free sandwich meats are easy to find. Tofu, a soy product that is high in protein and low in fat, is also readily available. Satisfy that sweet tooth with fat-free candies and fat-free chocolate, but do so in moderation: nothing in life is truly free. Too many fat-free cookies will cause weight gain because the excess sugar you've ingested will eventually convert to stored fat in your body.

## Chow Time Has Never Been So Good

Food fit for a dog now keeps dogs fit, frisky, and feeling fine. Research by veterinary nutritionists at major universities and commercial dog food firms has led to the creation of an ever-expanding array of pet foods with flavorful options that accommodate all ages, sizes, breeds, activity levels, and health conditions. Got an energetic beagle or a lazy Great Dane; a young golden retriever or an elderly Pekinese; a Doberman pinscher in need of immune system–boosting antioxidants or an arthritic German shepherd dog? No problem. On the pet food shelves or in your veterinarian's clinic are specially formatted foods that address many conditions, including obesity, cognitive dysfunction, and allergy sensitivities.

Lowell Ackerman, D.V.M., a Boston area veterinarian and author of more than 70 books, including *Canine Nutrition* (Alpine Publications, 1999), says the niche market for premium pet products is among the fastest growing and the most lucrative in the United States. As dogs become more important in our lives, we want to make sure that they get the best food possible. We are paying a lot of attention to what we put in our dogs' bowls because we are better educated than ever before, and we recognize the connection between food and health. We now know that proper nutrition can help a pet avoid many illnesses, and we know to avoid products that contains synthetic food preservatives.

Chow time has never been so good—both in providing taste and in addressing health needs. Today, commercial dog foods come in the following forms—each capable of providing complete and balanced nutrition:

**Dry:** Dry food is the easiest to store, generally the least expensive, and has the longest shelf life of all the dog foods. Most dry dog foods contain from 35 to 50 percent carbohydrates, from 18 to 27 percent protein, from 7 to 15 percent fat, and less than 12 percent moisture. High-quality dry foods list the animal-based protein as one of the first three ingredients. The crunchy kibble nuggets perform another role: they assist in preventing major buildup of tartar and plaque on dogs' teeth.

**Semi-Moist:** This food form delivers irresistible taste and a hamburger-like texture. In general, semi-moist dog food contains from 25 to 35 percent carbohydrates, from 16 to 25 percent protein, from 5 to 10 percent fat and about 30 percent water.

**Canned:** Ask any dog and she will tell you, paws down, that canned food rules! Bite for bite, it costs the most, but it provides the highest palatability. Brands vary, but the higher quality types list animal-based protein as one of the first two ingredients on the label. Most canned foods contain anywhere from 8 to 15 percent protein as well as 2 to 15 percent fat, and about 75 percent moisture. Once you open the can, you need to cover and store the unused portion in the refrigerator to keep it fresh.

How do you determine the amount of food to feed your dog? Start by referring to the general serving size guidelines provided on the food label. A small dog, for example, generally needs only 1 cup of chow but a giant breed may need 3 cups to meet her nutritional needs. And the amount of food can vary depending on a dog's situation; for example, pregnant or nursing females need more food than spayed females. Don't forget to factor in your dog's activity level. An energy-revved Jack Russell terrier requires more food than a lap-snoozing bichon frise—even though they weigh about the same—because the terrier burns more calories darting and dashing about.

Always use a measuring cup to dole out your dog's daily portions. Take the guesswork out of portion sizes by leveling off each scoop of food before pouring it into your dog's bowl. This provides you with a baseline. Also, weigh your adult dog every month; if your dog gains weight, you know to trim back on her portion size.

One healthy weight-loss strategy calls for adding more steamed vegetables to your dog's chow and less fatty meats. The vegetables are low in calories and help satisfy your dog's appetite so that she leaves the bowl feeling full. So add some healthy zest to your dog's commercial food—and take care of leftovers—by topping her kibble with steamed vegetables. Broccoli, green beans, and carrots are loaded with vitamins and minerals but contain no fat.

*Experiment in the kitchen to create healthy snacks for your dog and family.*

## Be a Healthy Chef for Your Chowhound

A generation ago we might have snickered at the notion of bakeries catering exclusively to dogs. But today, we unabashedly flock to places such as Three Dog Bakery or search the Internet for sites offering gourmet recipes and treats for our canines.

It's a good idea to give your dog an occasional break from commercial chow by serving up a homemade meal or treat that will cause her to drool with delight and beg for seconds: but resist giving her handouts. Now, I'm not suggesting that your dog tuck a napkin into her collar and join you at the dining room table, but periodically preparing homemade nutritious meals can improve your relationship with your dog. Plus, you can hone your cooking skills (why not try out a new recipe on your chowhound?).

Make sure that your homemade meals include a good portion of non-meat foods, especially grains, vegetables, and starches. Good sources of these foods include rice, bagels, oatmeal, tortillas, green beans, peas, broccoli, and spinach.

Practice the same hygiene habits when cooking for your dog that you do when cooking for you and your family. Prevent stomach upsets by:

- always washing your hands in warm soapy water and rinsing well before handling food;
- cleaning all produce in cold water to wash away pesticides, dirt, and bugs;
- trimming off fat and draining excess grease from cooked meats;
- choosing fresh ingredients, organically grown, if possible;
- cooking meat, seafood, poultry, and eggs thoroughly;
- providing fresh filtered water daily;
- storing leftovers in airtight containers in the refrigerator for no more than four days or freezing the leftovers in a container that you date and identify.

## Snack Time!

The mere mention of the word treat can send most dogs into a full-body wiggle. Adopt the motto Tricks for Treats. Mealtime and treat time make ideal training opportunities; take advantage of your dog's begging eyes by reinforcing obedience commands or introducing new tricks. A dog is willing to perform when she knows she will reap a delicious dividend.

Snacks quickly add up in calories, however, and are often overlooked as a source of your dog's walk turning into a waddle. When you count her calories, remember to factor in your dog's treats with her regular meals. And limit your dog's treats to no more than 10 percent of her total daily food portions.

One of my favorite treat tactics is to put one-fourth of my dog's daily kibble into the treat jar. When I reinforce her basic obedience commands or wish to praise her for mastering a new skill, I can grab a few pieces of kibble from the treat jar and, with great glee in my voice, I say, "Good job! Here's a treat for you." My dog eats the same amount of food each day, but a portion comes from that very special treat jar.

Other low-calorie treat options high in nutritional value that both you and your dog can enjoy together are air-popped popcorn, apple slices, raw baby carrots, and broccoli florets.

*Dogs love natural treats, like fresh apples and grapes.*

## Doggie Food Dangers

- **Death by chocolate.** This sweet treat can be downright deadly to your dog. Chocolate contains theobromine, a dangerous chemical that can cause severe, life-threatening diarrhea in dogs. Baking chocolate is especially harmful to dogs because it contains nearly nine times more theobromine than milk chocolate does. As little as 3 ounces of baking chocolate can kill a 25-pound dog. If you want to make a sweet treat for your dog, substitute carob for chocolate.

- **Onus on onions.** Onions contain a large amount of sulfur, which can destroy red blood cells and cause severe anemic reactions in dogs. The ingredients in onions can trigger diarrhea, vomiting, and fever. In small amounts, onions may be relatively safe for dogs to eat, but why take the risk?

- **The raw deal on real bones.** Meat bones harbor parasites and can splinter inside your dog's mouth or intestinal tract. They can cause vomiting, diarrhea, constipation, intestinal obstructions, and punctures. Select safer alternatives for those big soup bones or chicken legs; give your dog rawhide chew strips or nylon bones.

- **The milk menace.** A few occasional laps of milk from your cereal bowl may be okay, but don't serve your dog milk at every meal. Some dogs lack the enzyme lactase needed to break down the lactose (milk sugar) in milk and may suffer from diarrhea if they ingest it.

- **Oil and obesity.** One teaspoon of vegetable oil equals about 50 calories. For a small dog who needs only 300 calories a day to maintain her weight, one teaspoon of oil equals one-sixth of her total calories. Go easy on the sauces and oils in food preparation.

*Try making a home-cooked meal for your canine friend.*

## Bone Appetite for the Both of You

Let me offer you two quick-to-make recipes for a special occasion or as a tasty treat. Here comes the best news: these recipes earned paws-up approval by a leading veterinary nutritionist and the recipes are edible for both you and your dog!

These recipes are excerpted from my book, *Real Food for Dogs* (Storey Books, 2001). So, grab an apron—it's chow time!

### MARVELOUS MUTT MEATBALLS

*Have some fun and sharpen your dog's fetching skills by tossing her a few of these meatballs at dinnertime. And make a pot of spaghetti noodles for yourself.*

| | |
|---|---|
| 1/2 | pound ground lean beef |
| 1/3 | cup grated cheddar cheese |
| 1 | carrot, finely chopped and grated |
| 1/2 | cup bread crumbs |
| 1 | egg, whisked |
| 1 | teaspoon garlic powder |
| 1 | teaspoon tomato paste |

1. Preheat the oven to 350°F
2. Combine all ingredients in a medium-sized bowl
3. Scoop out by the spoonful and roll into mini meatballs
4. Place the meatballs on a cookie sheet sprayed with nonfat cooking spray
5. Bake for 15 to 20 minutes
6. Serve your meatballs hot on top of your pasta and cool a few before serving to your dog

### CANINE CASSEROLE

*Don't let this recipe's name dissuade you from having a helping or two.*

| | |
|---|---|
| 2 | cups brown rice, uncooked |
| 1/2 | pound ground chuck hamburger |
| 1 | teaspoon vegetable oil |
| 1 | garlic clove, crushed |
| 1/2 | cup finely chopped carrots |
| 1/2 | cup finely chopped broccoli |

1. Cook the rice in a steamer
2. Steam the carrots and broccoli until tender
3. Warm the vegetable oil in a pan over medium heat. Add the hamburger and garlic and sauté until cooked through
4. Combine all the ingredients
5. Serve your portion hot and allow your dog's portion to cool before serving. Store leftovers in the refrigerator in a sealed container.

### Success Spotlight: Trisha McKinney and Fred

Meet Fred, a 10-year-old Australian Shepherd who is crazy for ice cubes. Ever since he was a puppy, Fred's owner, Trisha McKinney of Washington, D.C., has given him ice cubes instead of bones as treats for good behavior.

"Fred will leap for an ice cube rather than a bone," says McKinney. "Our veterinarian thinks it's hysterical. But the ice cubes are calorie-free and easy on our wallets. At 10 years old, Fred doesn't gain extra doggy pounds and he is in great health."

# CHAPTER 4

* * * * * * * * *

# THE INSIDE SCOOP ON SUPPLEMENTS AND VITAMINS

* * * * * * * * *

The foods on your plate—and in your dog's bowl—may include all five food groups, but they may also be nutritionally incomplete. You can never, for example, obtain enough beta-carotene in your daily diet strictly by munching on carrots; you'd have to consume enough carrots to feed an army of rabbits. Should you reach for nutritional supplements? If so, which ones and in what amount and form?

Simply swallowing a pill, even a multivitamin, is no guarantee that you or your dog will stay fit and stave off diseases. Nutritional supplements—headlined by vitamins, minerals, herbs, and enzymes—should be used only to improve—not replace—a good diet. Used correctly, supplements can help maintain good health and even combat diseases and chronic conditions. Used incorrectly, they can be harmful, even deadly. Supplements should be added to your or your dog's diet only to compensate for a known nutrient deficiency such as calcium (as determined by a blood test) or maximize the amount of a certain nutrient to prevent a disease or to treat a chronic condition.

Before you head for the health food store or pet supply store and start plucking supplements off the shelf, consult with your physician or veterinarian to determine which supplements should be taken—and in what amount—to meet the special needs of either you or your dog.

Be careful. When it comes to supplements, the maxim "more is better" does not apply. If you give your dog too many calcium supplements, for example, you can cause harm to his joints and bones; too many copper or zinc supplements can be toxic.

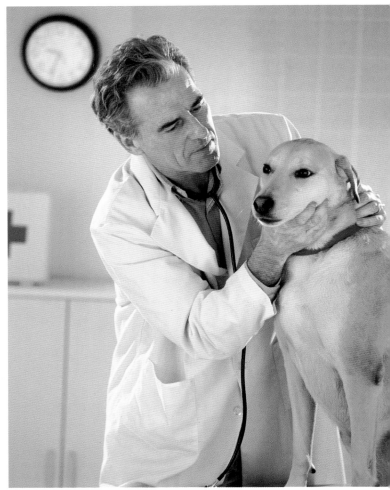

*Consult your vet about appropriate canine supplements.*

Before you buy, find answers to these key questions:

- Is this supplement safe?
- Can I afford it?
- What's the right dose to take?
- What's the best form (pill, powder, liquid)?
- Will it interfere with other medications that my dog or I am taking?

Fortunately, more and more physicians and veterinarians are paying attention to the possible health perks that nutritional supplements can offer. Two of my favorite health experts, Lowell Ackerman, D.V.M., a veterinarian from the Boston area, and Dale L. Anderson, M.D., a physician who is board certified in holistic medicine from Saint Paul, Minnesota, acknowledge that while supplements can bolster one's health, they are certainly not cure-alls.

"We have a lot to learn about supplements," says Dr. Ackerman. "We're just discovering that some nutrients have positive benefits beyond their nutritional claims. And, even if there isn't a dietary deficiency, taking supplements could possible serve as a good preventive against some diseases."

"We're seeing a lot of crossover in usage of supplements," notes Dr. Anderson. "It's not uncommon for a patient to ask me, 'The chondroitin and glucosamine that you recommended for me to take for my arthritis seems to be helping. Can I also give these supplements to my 10-year-old Labrador to ease the aches from the arthritis in his hips?' "

Both doctors agree that both humans and canines should take supplements only when neces-sary and only in the amount recommended by a health professional. If there is no noticeable improvement after a couple months, the supplements should be stopped.

## Doggone Good Vitamins

Vitamins fall into two camps: fat soluble and water soluble. Collectively, vitamins are multirole performers in the body. They interact with enzymes, convert calories to energy, assist in hormone production, and create blood cells. Here's a summary of 14 key vitamins for people and dogs and some of the foods that contain them:

*Supplements are not cure-alls.*

*Choose green, leafy vegetables and dairy products for essential vitamins.*

## FAT-SOLUBLE VITAMINS

**Vitamin A**—Important for vision, cell development, growth, and immunity. Major food sources: egg yolks, cantaloupes, carrots, broccoli, tomatoes, green beans, and liver

**Vitamin D**—Necessary for absorption of calcium; helps with bone building and nerve-muscle interaction. Major food sources: salmon, sardines, and fortified milk

**Vitamin E**—A major antioxidant, it helps protect cells and tissues from oxidation damage. Major food sources: kale, collards, fish, chili with beans, peanut butter, and shellfish

**Vitamin K**—This lesser-known vitamin helps regulate clotting in the blood. Major food sources: eggs, dairy products, fruits, and seeds

## WATER-SOLUBLE VITAMINS

**Vitamin C**— Helps build bones, teeth, and soft tissue, and it detoxifies the liver; it is also a key antioxidant. Major food sources: oranges, grapefruits, raw spinach, steamed broccoli, and sweet red peppers

**Folic Acid**—Necessary for growth and cell division; pairs up with Vitamin B12 in many chemical reactions in the body. Major food sources: liver, cold cereals, pinto beans, spinach, and broccoli

**Pantothenic acid**—Helps metabolize carbohydrates, fats, and protein, and it synthesizes neurotransmitters, which are necessary for energy. Major food sources: raw broccoli, avocados, bran, dry milk, and eggs

**Pyridoxine (Vitamin B$_6$)**—Major participant in metabolizing protein and amino acids. Major food sources: chicken, fish, whole-grain cereals, bananas, avocados, and egg yolks

**Cobalamin (Vitamin B$_{12}$)**—Necessary for DNA synthesis, cell division, and production of red blood cells. Major food sources: roast beef, bacon, ham, whole milk, and liver

**Biotin**—Assists in the synthesis and oxidation of fatty acids and the metabolism of several amino acids. Major food sources: peanut butter, egg yolks, cereals, nuts, cauliflower, and liver

**Niacin**—Essential for releasing energy from carbohydrates, fat, and protein. Major food sources: cereals, meats, and coffee

**Riboflavin (Vitamin B$_2$)**—Helps form red blood cells, releases energy from blood sugar, and promotes growth. Major food sources: milk, whole grains, fortified breads, broccoli, potatoes, orange juice, and liver

**Thiamin (Vitamin B$_1$)**—Metabolizes carbohydrates in the body and promotes a healthy appetite

Broccoli, red peppers, and tomatoes provide water-soluble vitamins.

---

## Pass the Carnitine, Please

Properly called L–carnitine, this vitamin-like amino acid is safe for both people and dogs. It plays a crucial role in cardiovascular metabolism and weight management, transporting fat into the mitochondria of the cell for energy consumption. Research shows that carnitine stimulates the rate of fat burning and increases the resting metabolic rate. Carnitine also promotes a leaner body by decreasing fat deposition in favor of muscle deposition. Even more importantly, carnitine serves as a storage system for fatty acids and helps fuel vital organs such as the heart.

Hill's Pet Nutrition was the first pet food company to verify the effects of carnitine on pet health. In 1998, the company added this supplement to its Prescription Diet Canine r/d and w/d formulas as a fat-burning nutrient to help overweight and obese dogs shed excess pounds by boosting fat metabolism and increasing lean muscle mass.

---

and growth. Major food sources: beans, whole grains, fortified breads, peas, and pork

**Choline**—Necessary for efficient nerve impulse transmission and keeping muscles strong. Major food sources: eggs, milk, liver, and beef. People and dogs need basically the same vitamins with one notable exception: vitamin C. Dogs, unlike us, makes their own vitamin C. This vitamin is at the heart of controversy in the dog world. Some breeders and veterinary researchers believe that supplementation may reduce the risk for hip dysplasia and other bone and joint problems in fast-growing breeds. But the majority of veterinary nutritionists say there is no scientific evidence to back this claim.

## Mighty Minerals

Minerals can be found in itty-bitty amounts in the tissues of all living animals, but they can carry a big punch. Balance is the key when it comes to minerals. When people or dogs are deficient in—or overloaded with—one or more mineral, their nutritional status and overall health can be jeopardized. For instance, too little iron can cause anemia, while too much calcium can block a human or canine body's ability to absorb and use other necessary minerals.

Two types of minerals are found in the body: major and trace minerals. The major minerals include calcium, phosphorus, magnesium, and sulfur. Topping the list of trace minerals are cobalt, copper, iodine, iron, manganese, selenium, and zinc. Let's look at the key minerals that promote good health in people and dogs:

**Calcium**—The most plentiful mineral in the body, calcium is crucial for bone formation, blood clotting, and neurotransmitter function. Major food sources: milk, cheese, yogurt, sardines, almonds, broccoli, green leafy vegetables, and soybeans

*Calcium can be found in such foods as milk and soy products.*

**Copper**—Rallies to aid T cells and antibodies in the immune system and helps protect against heart disease; also helps absorb iron. Major food sources: nuts, whole grain cereals, fruits, liver, and shellfish

**Cobalt**—Associated with vitamin $B_{12}$, cobalt helps form red blood cells and maintain nerve tissue. Major food sources: fruit, vegetables, liver, and kidney

**Iodine**—Critical for a healthy thyroid gland. Major food sources: fresh seafood, shellfish, and iodized salt

**Iron**—Acts like the body's taxicab by transporting oxygen and assisting in the formation of red blood cells; iron is found in every cell of the body. Major food sources: meat, fish, poultry, liver, apricots, potatoes, raw spinach, and raw broccoli

**Magnesium**—Necessary for muscle movement, conduction of nerve impulses, and protection against heart disease. Major food sources: nuts, seafood, vegetables, and dairy products

**Manganese**—Spurs enzymes that control nutrient metabolism. Major food sources: whole grain cereals, raisins, spinach, and wheat bran

**Phosphorus**—Complements calcium and is vital for bone growth and formation. Major food sources: yogurt, spinach, milk, and sweet potatoes

**Selenium**—The unheralded antioxidant, along with vitamins A, C, and E, selenium fights cancer, boosts the immune system, and helps the body detoxify metals. Too much selenium can harm the heart muscles, liver, and kidneys. Major food sources: organ meats, fish, cereals, dairy products, broccoli, and cucumbers

**Sulfur**—Helps ensure proper development of joint fluid and cartilage. Major food sources: meat, poultry, and fish

**Zinc**—Helps heal wounds, strengthen the immune system, and improve the senses of smell and taste; also promotes good coat health. Major food sources: lean beef, turkey, beans, cereal, and wheat germ

*Used wisely, herbs and supplements can complement your health.*

## Helpful Herbs

I've never been a great gardener, but I do constantly cultivate knowledge about the ultimate green pharmacy: medicinal herbs. Having coauthored *Herbs That Heal* (Rodale Press, 1999), attended international herbal conferences, and written about herbs for leading health publications, such as *Prevention* magazine, I maintain a healthy respect for the power of these botanicals.

As dogs deservedly become full-fledged members of households, more people are seeking natural, safe treatments for them. Following on the heels of the public's push into herbal medicines, caring dog owners have also begun to research the benefits of herbs for their canine pals. We want healthy options free of side effects often found in conventional medications. The attraction to herbs is understandable. This holistic therapy works at healing both the body and the mind. Herbal medicines strive to treat the underlying cause, not merely treat the symptoms. When used correctly, they can complement conventional treatment. That said, keep in mind that herbs are not cure-alls and should never be taken to replace doctor or veterinary care.

Always consult your dog's veterinarian before buying medicinal herbs. If your dog is on a prescribed medication, the herb could counter the effectiveness of the medication and worsen the condition. If you're unfamiliar with the fact that herbs come in different forms (including powders, tinctures, teas, and ointments), you may feel a bit confused, even conflicted, by all the available choices, so consider the following guidelines:

- **Treat botanical herbs like prescription drugs.** Although derived from plants, herbs can cause sickness—even death—if used improperly. For instance, willow bark works safely on dogs, but in large doses can be fatal to cats, because of their physiological differences.

- **Follow label directions.** Don't think more is better when it comes to herbal dosages. And never give a human dose to your dog. Of course, if your dog weighs over 100 pounds, he may require a

human dose, but always consult a holistic-trained veterinarian first to be safe. Some dosages for herbs are based on weight, but not all.

- **Introduce herbal medicines one at a time.** Evaluate the results of one herbal treatment before adding others. Some herbs work well together; others clash.

- **Work with your veterinarian.** Consult your veterinarian if you're trying to wean your dog off prescription medications and you are planning to introduce him to herbal treatment. If your dog is taking prescription medicines for behavior or chronic pain conditions, it's especially important to keep your veterinarian involved. In the long run, you could save money by switching to herbs and your dog might face fewer side effects from the medications.

- **Don't expect miracles or instant results.** Natural medicine is wonderful, but it is not a panacea, a cure-all, says Dr. Ackerman. It should never replace the need for diagnostic tests, or, when necessary, antibiotics, anesthesia, or surgery. You need to be patient and not expect instant results from taking medicinal herbs.

- **Be proactive**—not reactive—and seek a holistic veterinarian when your dog is still young and problem-free. Unfortunately, many holistic veterinarians treat dogs after the owner has exhausted all other options. If you start a young animal in natural medicine, you often can keep him healthy for many years.

## 10 HEALTHY HERBS FOR DOGS AND PEOPLE

Mother Nature offers a bounty of healing goodness with hundreds of herbs. Here are my personal picks of 10 herbs in alphabetical order that are effective and safe for you and your dog:

### Alfalfa (Medicago sativa)

**Uses:** For allergies, arthritis, cancer, cognitive disorder, and urinary disorders

**How it works:** Alfalfa contains chemicals that combat cancer and contains chlorophyll (an antioxidant), vitamin K, and digestive enzymes.

**Best form:** Fresh or powdered capsules

**Cautions:** Alfalfa is generally regarded to be a safe herb, but it is not recommended for people or dogs taking coumarin (an anticoagulant) because it may interfere with blood clotting.

*You can dry your own herbs at home.*

## Aloe (Aloe spp.)

**Uses:** For allergies (topical and herbal rinse), diarrhea (juice), cancer, minor cuts, wounds, insect bites, and infections

**How it works:** Prostaglandins inside the transparent gel deliver relief for minor sunburn, burns, skin irritations, cuts, scrapes, and poison ivy; aloe also contains special enzymes and antibacterial and antifungal ingredients that ease swelling, reduce redness, and fight infections.

**Best form:** Fresh. It is easy to grow an aloe plant in the house. When you need the herb, just snap off a lower leaf near the center stalk. Remove any spines and then split the leaf in half lengthwise. Squeeze its juice on the wound.

**Cautions:** Avoid ingesting aloe because it can act as a laxative and cause diarrhea.

It is not recommended for pregnant or lactating dogs or people, or for those diagnosed with liver or kidney disease.

## Catnip (Nepeta cataria)

**Uses:** As a mild sedative for restlessness, nervousness, or insomnia; also can relieve muscle spasms, diarrhea, gas, and minor respiratory problems

**How it works:** Long heralded among fans of felines, catnip is surprisingly effective on canines and people, too. The leaves and flowering tops of catnip, a member of the mint family, contain acetic acid, tannins, terpense, and volatile oils—plus vitamins A, B, and C.

**Best form:** Chopped up fresh leaves or crumbled dried leaves; can also be used externally as an antiseptic poultice for minor wounds and sores

**Cautions:** Generally considered safe with no side effects reported, but veterinarians recommend avoiding catnip for dogs under the age of 6 months. Humans who want to use catnip should, as is the case with any herb, check with the doctor first.

### Chamomile (Matricaria recutita, Chamaemelum nobile)

**Uses:** As a gentle sedative for anxiety, insomnia, and mild indigestion; also aids in the treatment of sore throats and inflamed eyes

**How it works:** This herb contains azulene (which kills staphylococcus and streptococcus infections) and chamazulene (which shrinks the swollen stomach tissue that causes pain by creating pressure on nerve endings).

**Best form:** Tea or tincture; the medicinal potency is found in the flowers

**Cautions:** Avoid using if you have allergies to closely related plants such as ragweed and chrysanthemums; do not give to pregnant dogs or women.

### Dandelion (Taraxacum officinale)

**Uses:** For allergies, arthritis, cancers, constipation, diabetes, kidney disease, liver disease, mild pain, and urinary disorders; also can be used as a diuretic

**How it works:** This common lawn weed, especially the roots and leaves, acts as a natural cleansing tonic for the liver. The most active ingredients—eudesmanolide and germacranolide—are found in the root. Dandelion also contains vitamins A, B, C, and E, plus potassium, calcium, and iron to act as a tonic for the urinary system and liver.

*Many herbs can be steeped into healthful tea.*

**Best form:** Fresh; select young leaves and roots from places you know are free of pesticides and other harmful chemical sprays

**Cautions:** Generally safe but not recommended for people or dogs with bile duct or gallbladder disorders; dandelion acts as a diuretic so make sure to give yourself and your dog plenty of bathroom breaks.

### Tea (Camellia sinensis)

**Uses:** As an immune system booster and heart protector; it also fights stomach and skin cancers

**How it works:** A popular hot drink, tea contains polyphenols and catechins, compounds that protect the heart by lowering cholesterol. They also act as powerful antioxidants and are believed to be part of the cancer-fighting army. Tea is loaded with vitamin C and caffeine, which rev up the metabolism.

**Best form:** Brewed as a tea. Sip your cup of tea while it's warm, but let it cool before pouring it over your dog's dry food.

**Cautions:** none

## Ginkgo (Ginkgo biloba)

**Uses:** As a memory booster and for antiaging; also fights dementia and depression and fortifies the nervous and cardiovascular systems

**How it works:** Active ingredients terpene lactones and flavone glycosides work to improve circulation and enhance elasticity of blood vessels.

**Best form:** Pill or capsule form, tincture

**Cautions:** Consult your physician or veterinarian before taking ginkgo if you or your dog are taking blood thinners; do not give to dogs diagnosed with hypertension or kidney disease.

## Licorice (Glycyrrhiza glabra)

**Uses:** Combats arthritis, asthma, coughs, and congestion; soothes the digestive system and acts as a diuretic

**How it works:** Licorice contains glycyrrhizin, known as nature's cortisone for its anti-inflammatory abilities; other compounds in licorice boost the immune system and kill germs.

**Best form:** Tea or tincture made from the root

**Cautions:** Do not use continuously or if you or your dog have been diag-nosed with diabetes, high blood pressure, or liver or kidney disease.

## Milk thistle (Silybum marianum)

**Uses:** For liver ailments, including cirrhosis and hepatitis; also promotes milk secretion in lactating female dogs and humans

**How it works:** A potent antioxidant, milk thistle contains flavolignans, essential oils, and mucilage that treat liver diseases; these chemicals are believed to hasten cell regeneration in damaged liver tissue.

**Best form:** Tincture or capsule

**Cautions:** Generally safe but can cause mild diarrhea in large amounts; do not give to pregnant women or dogs.

*Practically any herb can be ingested in capsule form.*

**Slippery elm (Ulmus rubra formerly known as Ulmus fulva)**

**Uses:** Eases diarrhea and nervous stomachs; also fights infection, reduces inflammation, and treats sore throats, coughs, and minor cuts

**How it works:** Tannins in this herb reduce inflammation; oily mucilage chemicals help in waste elimination and act as lubricants for the digestive tract.

**Best form:** A topical for wounds and abscesses and a tincture or capsule for other ailments

**Cautions:** Do not use continuously; do not give to pregnant dogs or people.

## Other Key Supplements

**Ask me about acidophilus.** Do you—or your dog—have frequent bouts of gas or diarrhea? The nutritional supplement acidophilus is a beneficial bacteria that helps detoxify and fortify the digestive tract. It is a probiotic often recommended during post-surgery recovery, when taking certain medications (including antibiotics and steroids), and at other times when the body's normal flora of the bowel region gets disrupted. The next time you eat yogurt, take a closer peek at the label and you will see that lactobacillus acidophilus is included.

*Yogurt is a good source of acidophilus, which can aid digestion.*

*Many herbs, like ginkgo, help fight depression.*

**Feast on brewer's yeast.** Itch, itch, scratch, scratch. Make fleas flee with brewer's yeast, a high-protein nutritional supplement that is loaded with B vitamins, key amino acids, and phosphorus. Sprinkle on your food and in your dog's bowl to bolster your immune systems. This is generally a safe supplement, but veterinarians caution against giving it to growing puppies or to senior dogs because of the large amounts of phosphorus.

**Clues about coenzyme Q ($C_oQ_{10}$).** Although, chemically, this nutrient resembles a vitamin, it is not one. $C_oQ_{10}$ can be found in all animals, plants, and microbes; edible sources include salmon, sardines, and fresh mackerel. This vital antioxidant is gaining popularity among people looking for ways to help themselves and their dogs with heart disease, high blood pressure, weak immune systems, allergies, and cancer. Does $C_oQ_{10}$ work? At this point, there is no scientific evidence of its effectiveness, but researchers view it as a safe nutrient.

**The chondroitin-glucosamine combination.** Aching joints, sore muscles, and arthritis can make us and our dogs feel older. Relief can be found by partnering these two supplements, chondroitin and glucosamine, which are touted to ease the aches and limited mobility associated with arthritis—minus any serious side effect. They also may help make cartilage less brittle.

**Fishy facts.** Essential fatty acids found in fish, namely omega-3 and omega-6, deliver natural anti-inflammatory benefits and are recommended for treating allergies, cancer, diabetes, heart disease, and kidney disease. They also help give your dog a shiny coat. Follow the recommended dose because too much can cause diarrhea and other digestive upsets. Flaxseed oil can also be used in place of fish.

Qualified holistic veterinary practitioners are located throughout the United States. For local referrals, consider contacting the American Holistic Veterinary Medical Association, based in Bel Air, Maryland, at its web site: www.altvetmed.com. Founded in 1982, this group provides a referral service of its active members and offers continuing education seminars for practicing veterinarians.

## Solid Sources for Info on Supplements

Visit the National Institutes of Health Office of Dietary Supplements on-line at http://dietary-supplements.info.nih.gov/for information about ingredients in supplements. Or check the Supplement Quality (www.supplementquality.com) Web site, which provides accurate information on standards and regulations for supplements, safety issues, and tips on how to read product labels.

## Selecting a Qualified Holistic Practitioner for Your Pet

Herbal medicines are only one component of a practice for a holistic health practitioner or holistic-trained veterinarian. The other types of holistic practices may include the use of therapeutic massage, vitamin B injections, yoga, and other modalities aimed at healing the body and soothing the mind. Chose a veterinarian or holistic health practitioner based on the responses to these questions:

✔ What are your qualifications in holistic medicine? Was it a weekend course or a 150-hour continuing education course that required you to pass a practical test in order to be certified?

✔ How long have you been practicing holistic medicine? What got you interested in it?

✔ What is your success rate? Have you expanded your practice, been asked to speak at conferences, etc.?

✔ Do you belong to any holistic veterinary medicine professional group and are you an active member?

✔ Would you be willing to provide names and telephone numbers of your clients?

✔ Are you willing to discuss my pet's case with the veterinarian who provides him primary conventional care?

✔ Will you take the time to explain holistic concepts to me and explain any possible side effects or safety issues related to the holistic medicine or technique you recommend for my pet?

## Success Story: Michael and Kathleen Rosenberg and Henry

Perhaps the most famous member of this New York City family is Henry, a four-year-old soft-coated wheaten terrier. You may recognize his famous face—it appears on some food bags for the Ralston Purina Company and even on banner advertisements on New York City buses. But Henry and his owners, Michael and Kathleen Rosenberg, take it all in stride—literally. They stay in shape by running together in Central Park, often running five miles with Henry stopping only occasionally to ham it up when he spots a camera. "If a tourist in Central Park is photographing someone or something, Henry will sit and pose," laughs 74-year-old Michael Rosenberg, who, with Kathleen, have completed eight marathons together. Henry stayed home for those 26.2-mile efforts.

"We never had any injuries running and I attribute that, in part, to doing warm-ups and cool downs," says Rosenberg. "When Kathleen and I stretch, it's doggy see, doggy do with Henry. He will stretch on his own. He's a terrific dog and an excellent running partner."

# CHAPTER 5

✦ ✦ ✦ ✦ ✦ ✦ ✦ ✦ ✦

# LET'S GET PHYSICAL

✦ ✦ ✦ ✦ ✦ ✦ ✦ ✦ ✦

Say the word exercise and many people respond with one word: Ugh. Or they may come up with a half-dozen excuses why they can't make it to the gym or reasons why their bike gathers cobwebs in the garage.

Try replacing the word exercise with motion. The magic of motion is that you don't need to participate in an Iditarod with your dog to reap healing benefits. Each time you lift, bend down, twist, turn, throw, walk, run, or even skip, you're improving your digestion, melting away body fat, and fortifying your body against a host of medical woes, including certain cancers, diabetes, gastrointestinal upsets, and heart problems.

Keeping your body in motion is like putting gold in the bank. A national study by the American Heart Association reported that burning 2,000 calories a week by performing a physical activity—such as walking an hour a day for a week—could increase life expectancy by two full years. Another study at Stanford reported that every hour spent in vigorous exercise as an adult is rewarded with two hours added to that person's life span. Try stepping up your daily physical activity in small increments. Star with a ten-minute walk around the block, which will make your joints more limber, muscles stronger, and mind happier.

Dale L. Anderson, M.D., a fit physician from Saint Paul, Minnesota, and Liz Palika, a terrific dog trainer from Oceanside, California, team up to identify 10 benefits of exercising with your dog:

- You perk up your postures and fortify your bones.
- You enhance your immune systems to protect both of you against infections.
- You reduce your risk for many joint and back pains.
- You can s-l-o-w down your aging process.
- You increase the strength of the bond between you and your dog.
- You improve the communication between you and your dog through exercise.
- Your minds become stimulated to make thinking easier and learning better.
- Your dog is less apt to develop behavior problems due to boredom, separation anxiety, or bottled-up energy.
- You and your dog can meet friends who are also interested in outdoor activities.
- Regular exercise that unleashes the body's endorphins and other feel-good chemicals can be as effective as prescription drugs in combating stress, anxiety, and depression.

## S-t-r-e-t-c-h Your Limbs

Both you and your dog need to begin each activity with a five-minute warm-up to stretch your muscles. To help your canine stretch, use a treat for motivation, and have her jump up on you to stretch her back muscles. If your dog is a jumper by nature, only practice the jump stretch when using a verbal command so the dog does not get confused. Then have her get into a play bow (outstretched front legs, head down low and rear end up high) to stretch her front muscles. Then, place your dog on her side and gently but firmly stretch each of her legs, one at a time. Hold each leg stretch

*Try some simple games to get your dog to stretch before a walk.*

for five seconds before releasing. If willing and able, have your dog do a figure eight pattern in between and around your legs, a natural limbering maneuver.

And don't forget yourself. Neglecting to stretch is one of the biggest mistakes people make while trying to get in shape. Stretching helps your body perform better because your muscles are warmed and you gain a greater range of motion. There is also a psychological boost to stretching: relaxed muscles transmit messages to your brain that everything is okay.

Selene Yeager, a certified fitness trainer and triathlete from Emmaus, Pennsylvania, offers some points on limbering up.

Muscles, in people or dogs, need to have some blood pumping through them and be warm before they can be stretched safely and effectively. Try jumping rope, running in place, or doing some light calisthenics for a few minutes before stretching.

Stretch only to the point where you feel gentle tension, then stop and hold the stretch. Stop if you feel pain.

Move slowly and steadily and avoid bouncing movements while you stretch. Hold each stretch 10 to 30 seconds.

Breathe deeply during your stretches. Do not hold your breath.

Not sure what or how to stretch? Try these all-time favorites, holding each stretch for about 20 seconds:

## ARMS OVERHEAD

Stand with your feet shoulder width apart and your head facing directly forward and your arms at your sides. Slowly lift your arms directly over your head while still looking forward. Do not arch your back. When your arms are directly overhead, lace your fingers together with your palms facing upward. Hold that up-to-the-sky reach then slowly drop your arms to your sides.

## BE NICE TO YOUR NECK

Do this stretch either standing or sitting. Keep your eyes facing forward and your back straight as you slowly let your head fall toward your left shoulder. Stop and hold for 10 to 20 seconds. Slowly bring your head back to its original position and then drop your head slowly toward your right shoulder. Hold that stretch up to 20 seconds before releasing.

*Stretch until you feel a gentle tension.*

*Many techniques allow you to stretch more than one muscle group, such as the back and legs.*

### PALM A WALL

Stand at arm's length from a wall and place your palms flat against it at shoulder height. Extend your right leg about 3 feet behind you and press your right heel to the floor. Keep both heels flat against the floor as you hold this stretch for 20 seconds. Return to the starting position and do this same stretch with your left leg.

### GET A LEG OUT

Sit on the floor and extend your right leg straight out and keep it flexed. Position your left leg so that the sole of your left leg touches your right inner thigh. Keep your back straight and your eyes facing forward. Slowly bend down from the waist and move your hands toward your right ankle. Hold that stretch for 20 seconds. Switch legs and repeat.

*Dogs are natural yoga masters, using classic movements in their everyday posture.*

## Yoga, Doggy Style

Everyday stretches are certainly helpful, but if you're interested in staying (or becoming) flexible, take notes the next time your dog goes through her stretching routine; dogs are natural yoga masters. Students of this ancient Eastern exercise didn't overlook the dog's purposeful movements: two classic yoga poses (or asanas) are named for canines.

Joely Johnson, a certified yoga instructor from Philadelphia, offers two doggone good yoga poses. One caution: if you have neck or back problems, please check with your doctor before trying these exercises. For best results, do these poses in front of a mirror and practice the posture daily with your dog, if possible. And don't be surprised if your own "tail" wags a little easier:

- **Downward Facing Dog:** In Sanskrit, this pose is called adho mukha svanasana. Place a yoga or exercise mat on the floor. Position your hands and knees on the mat. Walk your hands out one hand's length. Place your palms on the floor and spread your fingers evenly. The middle fingers should parallel one another. Straighten your legs and lift your buttocks and torso upward, pushing strongly into your hands as you do this. Reach your tailbone higher than your hips. Imagine opening the backs of your knees as you stretch your heels toward the floor. Keep pushing your hands away from you, stretching through your shoulders and shoulder blades. Keep your face and neck relaxed and breathe deeply through your nose. Take five deep breaths then slowly return to your hands and knees.

- **Upward Facing Dog:** In Sanskrit, this pose is called urdhva mukha svanasana. Start by lying face down on a mat or towel. Rest your forehead on the floor, place your palms down next to your shoulders and tuck your elbows close to your sides. Your toes should be gently pointing away from you and the tops of your feet should be on the floor. Put the weight into your hands as you lift your head and torso. Begin to straighten your arms but remember to keep your elbows in. Push down on your feet, keeping your legs straight. Continue to straighten your arms until your torso is fully lifted. Keeping your shoulders down, lift your chin up as you drop your head back, completing the backward bend. Take five deep breaths in this position, then bring your head back to center, tuck your toes under, and return to your hands and knees.

## The Magic of Massage

Equally important to stretching is the power of a purposeful touch. Whenever a good friend gives me a neck rub, my first word is "ah" because her fingers knead and press away the snarl of knots created by my being hunched over a laptop computer.

Therapeutic massage knows no age—or species—boundaries. The kneading, pressing, and circular massage motions help untie muscle knots, unleash tension, and increase flexibility in people and their pets.

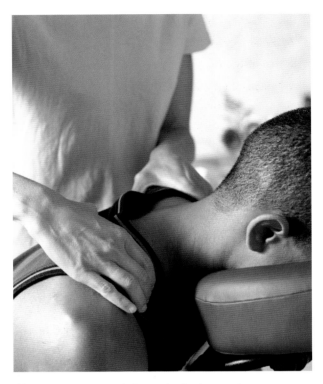

*Massage improves circulation and unleashes tension.*

"Once you learn massage, you'll never pet your dog the same way again," says C. Sue Furman, Ph.D., an associate professor of anatomy and neurobiology at Colorado State University and a canine and equine massage therapy instructor from Windsor, Colorado.

There hasn't been much research done on therapeutic touch for dogs, but we're heading in that direction as more people are getting interested in learning massage. Think of massage as a purposeful touch to your dog—much more than petting. You are using your hands and fingers in ways to promote health. Performed properly, massage can generate many physical and mental benefits for your dog. For example, canine massage:

- warms body tissues;
- improves joint flexibility;
- soothes tight muscles;
- promotes healthy skin and coat;
- improves blood flow and lymphatic circulation;
- removes toxins and wastes from the body;
- relaxes and calms;
- improves your dog's sleep;
- conditions your dog to being touched;
- reduces symptoms associated with arthritis and other chronic conditions;
- speeds surgical recovery;
- improves socialization in puppies and animal shelter dogs;
- curbs behavioral problems such as destructive chewing;
- tightens friendship and trust bonds between you and your dog.

Dogs need massages on a regular basis. Typically, dogs will overdo it when trying to please you. Since they don't know how to say no, they can pull muscles and injure themselves. Performing canine massages regularly also helps you detect any lumps or body changes early.

As beneficial as massage can be, it shouldn't be regarded as a cure-all or a replacement for traditional care such as medication or surgery, cautions Dr. Furman, author of *Balance Your Dog: Canine Massage* (Wolfchase Publishing, 2003). Massage can heal, but, if performed incorrectly, it can also cause more harm than good. Never massage over an open wound, broken bone, or surgical spot.

## THE REAL RUB ON MASSAGE

Holistic veterinarians and animal massage therapists offer these top 10 dos and don'ts to novice dog masseurs:

**DO**

- make sure your dog permits the massage; find a time when she will appreciate it;
- give your dog your full attention;
- wash your hands before administering the massage;
- massage with your hands and never your feet;
- make slow, deliberate movements;
- move in the direction toward the heart;
- work your way up to half-hour massages;
- focus on feedback signs from your dog;
- remember strokes and favorite massage areas on your dog and repeat them;
- use this time to check your dog's body for fleas and ticks, cuts, scratches, lumps, or swellings and report any concerns to your veterinarian.

## Key Strokes and Hand Positions

Animal massage therapists identify the following basic hand positions and motions:

✔ **Open hand:** With palm side facing down, apply gentle pressure in long, flowing strokes from head to tail.

✔ **Curved hand:** Relaxed palms and fingers move evenly over curved contours in long, flowing strokes.

✔ **Thumb walk:** Apply direct, gentle pressure with the thumbs on your dog's specific trigger points. Such areas include around the eyes, skull, ears, and either side of the spine.

✔ **Clasp hands:** Interlace fingers of both hands with palms facing up. Slide the hands underneath the dog's chest and abdomen and gently pull upward, then hold and slowly lower.

✔ **Finger circles:** Use the tip of your fingers (never your fingernails) and make small tight circles on your dog's muscles; work clockwise and counterclockwise.

✔ **Effleurage:** The most basic massage stroke, effleurage combines simple touch with light friction and movement. Strokes are slow, long, flowing, and even-pressured.

✔ **Compression:** This stroke presses into the dog's body using the thumbs, fingers, and palms of one or both hands. This is a motion similar to gently squeezing water from a damp sponge.

✔ **Joint rotation:** Support your dog's body with one hand while you grab a leg joint with the other hand. Slowly move the leg back and forth and then in a circular motion to increase flexibility. Don't forget the tail.

✔ **Tapping:** With an open hand, softly tap your fingertips on your dog at a rate of three to four taps per second per area.

✔ **Skin rolling:** This motion involves grabbing and lifting the coat and skin away from muscles, bones, and fat to provide a healthy stretch to the connective tissue; make rhythmic, rolling movements and avoid pinching.

✔ **Vibration:** Move your hand or fingers rapidly back and forth over your dog's body.

*Set aside a special time to perform a gentle massage on your dog.*

## DON'T

- force a massage on a dog;
- attempt a massage when you're harried or hurried; your dog reads your body cues;
- press too deeply—you could harm your dog;
- use oils, creams, or lotions;
- provide a massage immediately after mealtime—wait at least 30 minutes;
- wake your dog from a sound sleep to perform a massage;
- continue massaging an area if you feel your dog trembling or shaking internally;
- massage directly on open wounds, blisters, abrasions, or recent surgical areas;
- substitute massage for medical care for arthritis—massage should complement the treatment plan outlined by your veterinarian;
- massage your dog if she has a fever.

## Try the Tellington Touch

Nearly 40 years ago, a spirited woman named Linda Tellington-Jones first gained fame for her uncanny ability to communicate with and calm problem horses. She discovered that her therapeutic approach, known as the TTouch, could also treat physical, emotional, and behavioral problems in family pets.

So what is TTouch? Tellington-Jones describes it as "the touch that teaches." The therapy involves circular movements of the fingers and hands all over the body. But the work is not magic. It is based on the scientific notion that the nervous system is connected to the brain and that tension, fear, and pain held in the body keep an animal from functioning fully.

To do the TTouch, make clockwise circles with lightly curved fingers on the skin. Maintain a steady rhythm and constant pressure as you glide your fingers clockwise 1 1/4 revolutions. There are nine degrees of pressure with the lightest being one.

## Why Use TTouch?

TTouch provides physical, mental, and emotional benefits to dogs, cats, horses, and other animals. A sampling of its therapeutic uses includes:

**Physical benefits:**
- ✔ relieving arthritis and muscle stiffness
- ✔ easing carsickness
- ✔ increasing circulation and digestion
- ✔ taming hyperactivity
- ✔ soothing pain from hip dysplasia and back problems
- ✔ improving gait and balance
- ✔ speeding healing and surgical recovery
- ✔ addressing flea and skin allergies and hot spots

**Mental benefits:**
- ✔ increasing a dog's willingness to learn
- ✔ building self-confidence for show competition
- ✔ strengthening the bond between owner and dog

**Behavioral benefits:**
- ✔ quieting excessive barking
- ✔ curbing fear biting and aggressiveness
- ✔ stopping leash pulling
- ✔ stopping constant jumping on people
- ✔ addressing phobias such as fear of loud noises or thunderstorms

Always select a quiet time for you and your dog and limit each session to 10 to 30 minutes. Maintain calm, deep breathing.

### BASIC TTOUCH TECHNIQUES

Tellington-Jones created nine different moves, many named in celebration of animals. Here are some of the more common TTouches and their benefits:

**1. Ear TTouch:** This is the most basic and essential technique, developed because several key acupuncture points correlating to different parts of the body and bodily function are located on the ears. It is used to help a dog relax, combat stress, improve digestion, relieve carsickness, and treat shock.

**The steps:** Make tiny circles between your thumb and forefinger and cover your dog's entire ear region in long glides. Then work tiny circles with your fingertips on the tips of your dog's ears.

**2. Clouded Leopard:** The name describes how your hand rests on your dog's body. The pressure should be as light as a cloud. This technique is used to treat aggression, excessive barking, carsickness, leash pulling, nervousness, stress, and to build self-confidence.

**The steps:** Place the weight of your hand lightly on your dog's body, with your fingers lightly curved. Use the pads of your fingers to push down lightly on your dog's skin and make a quarter circle. The middle finger should lead. Keep your forefinger and thumb about 1 1/2 to 2 inches apart and your wrist straight and flexible. Be sure to move the skin in a circle rather than rub over the hair.

**3. Tarantulas Pulling the Plow:** This unusually named technique is a comforting way to introduce TTouch to fearful dogs or older dogs sensitive to being touched. It is best used to increase circulation, to treat emotional or grooming problems, and to combat pain.

**The steps:** Place your hands side by side with the fingertips separated and curved slightly. The thumbs, lightly touching each other, should lag behind your fingers as you "wall" the forefingers and middle fingers across the grain of your dog's hair. Allow your thumbs to follow behind, pushing a light furrow of hair along, just like a plow in a field.

**4. Mouth TTouch:** This technique affects your dog's emotional and physical states and sharpens her ability to focus and learn. Try this movement on dogs who bark or lick excessively, chew, bite, or act hyper. The technique helps a dog relax, allowing her, for example, to tolerate dental work and veterinary exams much better.

**The steps:** Sit behind your dog and support her chin muzzle in one hand. Slide back and forth on the outside and inside of her lips and make tiny circles on the gums with your fingertips from the hand that is not supporting the muzzle. Work both sides of the mouth. Use gentle but steady pressure.

**5. Tail TTouch:** Strange as it sounds, you may be able to alleviate your dog's fear of loud noises and thunderstorms as well as address her temper, gait, back and balance problems, arthritis, and aggression by working her tail region. This movement brings about awareness and attention to the dog's hindquarters.

**The steps:** Lift your dog's tail, making a straight line from her body. Stroke downward on the tail several times to get your dog used to being touched. With one hand at the base of the tail, slowly create an arch by pushing the tail upward and in a clockwise circular motion. Then rotate counterclockwise several times. Finish by working small circles all the way down the tail. Some dogs with docked tails may have sensitivity around the tail area, so this exercise may not be comfortable for them.

---

### Success Story: Karen Claborn and Bear

What distinguishes Karen Claborn from other folks in her Brea, California, neighborhood is that she carries a big shovel when she walks Bear, her 12-year-old, 140-pound landseer Newfoundland.

The 5-pound, wooden-handled, steel-bladed shovel does more than scoop poop. Claborn, a high school history teacher, uses the shovel to tone her arms and upper back muscles in between Bear's "deposits."

"I lift the shovel above my head, hold it directly out in front of me and then behind me, and use it like a weight to exercise my arms as I walk Bear," says Claborn. "My neighbors kid me, but I don't mind. Since I began 'working out' with the shovel on my walks a couple years ago, my arms are much more toned and my back muscles feel great. I used to go to a gym but this is a much better— and free—way to exercise."

# CHAPTER 6

⋆ ⋆ ⋆ ⋆ ⋆ ⋆ ⋆ ⋆ ⋆

# FUN WITH FITNESS—ANYTIME, ANYWHERE

⋆ ⋆ ⋆ ⋆ ⋆ ⋆ ⋆ ⋆ ⋆

Your tail-wagger bounds your way, does a belly roll, and gives a friendly yelp. He then postures into a play bow with his front paws extended out and his head tucked into his chest. Finally, he looks right at you and you swear that his eyes are actually twinkling. How can you resist this invitation to play? And, why would you?

Dogs didn't invent fun, but they definitely put the P in play. They offer us relief from a world of gridlock, mortgages, and work deadlines. Allowing your dog's contagious, carefree spirit to infect you will put you in a better mood and find you smiling more.

The beauty of playtime with your dog is that it can occur anytime, anywhere. Your dog doesn't require your people to contact his people to book an appointment. For the most part, he doesn't need special equipment. He's usually ready and raring to go at the drop of a leash. Whether his playtime is five minutes or an hour, your dog will always be content to interact with you.

## Calorie-Burning Activities

The opportunities for people to burn calories are endless. You may be surprised by how many—or how few—calories are expended. Listed below is a chart that identifies some common people activities. The numbers provided below are based on a 140-pound person performing each of these activities for an hour. Use this chart as a baseline for you:

| Activity | Calories burned |
| --- | --- |
| Backpacking | 445 |
| Biking | 509 |
| Canoeing | 255 |
| Cleaning the garage | 255 |
| Cleaning the house | 159 |
| Gardening | 318 |
| Jogging | 445 |
| Mountain biking | 541 |
| Playing tag with a dog or kids | 318 |
| Running | 700 |
| Shoveling snow | 382 |
| Stretching | 159 |
| Swimming | 509 |
| Trail walking | 318 |
| Walking the dog | 191 |

*Aerobic activities like biking burn hundreds of calories per hour.*

*Some dogs are built for running, while others are better suited to steady-paced walking.*

## Canine Conditioning

Before you lace your sneakers and grab the leash for that outdoor romp, schedule an appointment with your veterinarian to give your dog a head-to-tail physical. Discuss the best optimal workout plan for your pooch based on his health, age, body shape, likes, and dislikes.

No two dogs are the same. An exercise routine may work for one dog but not for another, even if they are the same breed. Generally, long-legged, light-framed dogs are best suited for jogging and leaping while short-legged, stocky-framed dogs are built for short energy bursts and steady-paced walks. But there are always the exceptions: for example, the golden retriever who prefers long, loping walks or the low-to-the-ground basset hound who craves a spirited half-mile jog.

As a general guideline, the average adult dog benefits by receiving 20–45 minutes of moderate exercise a day, such as a brisk walk. Gradually build up your dog's aerobic capacity by starting with a brisk five-minute walk. Or engage in short 5- to 10-minute play sessions with your dog. Roll a ball across the backyard for him to chase, for example. Just like you, your dog needs time to get into condition to be able to safely exercise for 30 minutes or more. Set realistic goals that match your dog's needs and abilities, not your personal wishes. You need to condition your dog at his pace rather than push him to meet your people- or ego-defined goals.

Finally, be consistent with your exercise regime. Don't turn your dog into a weekend warrior—a canine who exercises only on Saturdays and Sundays. He is apt to injure himself. Reduce that risk by letting him burn off some calories every-day—even if only for 20 minutes.

### Take the TV Test

Is your dog exercising too much or too little? Suzanne Clothier, a professional dog trainer and breeder from St. Johnsville, New York, gets her answer on any night that she watches prime time television shows. A dog craving more exercise will often get in between you and the television show you are attempting to watch. A bone-tired dog, however, will flop on the floor and barely move even during a noisy show. A dog who receives adequate exercise will sit by your side, lightly snoozing or contently chewing on a bone.

### Dog-Tired Signs

Dogs are such pleasers that they won't tell you when they're too tired to go on. It's up to you to read their cues. Take a break and stop the activity if you notice any of these signs in your dog:

- ✔ drooping tongue
- ✔ rapid panting—an early sign of overheating
- ✔ hesitation—taking a few extra seconds before retrieving a tossed ball
- ✔ weight shifting—using different muscle groups to offset soreness
- ✔ staggered walking
- ✔ muscle tremors

### Walk this Way

You and your dog were made for walking. The simple act of putting one foot (or paw) in front of the other can burn off calories and tone muscles without jarring the joints and bones. You both will improve your cardiovascular health and lose the waddle from your walk. Ensure that walk time is safe and fun for the both of you by paying attention to the weather and your surroundings.

Let's start first with a popular walking surface, the sidewalk. Remember that we wear soled shoes or sneakers, but our dogs go barefoot. On warm sunny days, test the sidewalk temperature before your dog steps foot on the concrete or asphalt surface. Place your palm on the sidewalk to test its heat intensity. If it's too warm to your touch, steer your dog toward grassy surfaces, or time your walks in the early morning or in the evening to protect your dog's footpads.

*Choose a natural walking surface to protect your dog's foot pads.*

On wintry days, avoid sidewalks treated with salt, magnesium, or calcium chloride. These ice-melting chemicals can irritate your dog's feet and cause an upset stomach if ingested. If you fit your dog with booties (and if he tolerates them), make sure they fit snugly but not tight enough to cut off circulation. Once you return home, wipe off your dog's feet with a damp towel. And for your sidewalk and driveway, consider using a nontoxic, pet-friendly ice melter.

## Size Up Your Dog for Winter Activities

Canine clothing can help insulate and draw away moisture from the skin of your thin-coated dog during severely cold days. Make sure the clothing covers any bald areas on the chest or belly.

Not sure how to size up your dog to select the right sweater? Take a cloth tape measure and wrap it around your dog's chest at his widest point, right behind the front legs. Here's a handy measurement chart to help you select the right size for your dog:

| Clothing | Chest measurement | Size |
|---|---|---|
| Sweater | 12" and under | XS |
| | 14–15" | S |
| | 16–17" | M |
| | 19–20" | L |
| | 21–22" | XL |
| | 23"-plus | XXL |
| | | |
| Canine coat | 12" and under | XS |
| | 12–14" | S |
| | 15–17" | M |
| | 18–20" | L |
| | 21–23" | XL |
| | 24–25" | XXL |
| | 26"-plus | XXXL |

No matter the weather, always keep your eyes open for vehicles, people, dogs, and other possible distractions on your route. When you spot potential trouble or temptation, switch directions or put your dog into a sit command to avoid any confrontations.

Do you walk the dog or does your dog walk you? If you have a four-legged leash-tugger or one who likes to zip around and get you all tangled in the leash, there's a simple solution: invest in a head halter, a Gentle Leader, Halti, or Softee. These collars are more effective and humane than choke or pinch collars and they allow you to control your dog's head, which, in turn, controls his body direction. These collars have special fitting requirements, so pay close attention at the pet store when you purchase one. During walks, reward your dog whenever there is slack in the leash; refuse to continue the walk when he starts to pull.

Keep your dog's attention by making yourself a bigger prize in his eyes than squirrels, cats, or overflowing trash cans. How? Stash a few yummy treats or your dog's favorite toy in your jacket before you head out the door. Periodically during your walk, call your dog by name and as soon as he turns to look at you, reward him with a treat or a quick game of fetch. Your dog will soon learn that it is more rewarding to pay attention to you than to that cat or soda can. He will also learn who's in charge.

## CALORIE CALCULATIONS

The more you walk and the faster the pace, the more weight you can take off for good.

| Your weight | Pace | Calories burned (1 hour) |
|---|---|---|
| 125 | 2 mph | 156 |
| | 3 mph | 251 |
| 140 | 2 mph | 174 |
| | 3 mph | 288 |
| 160 | 2 mph | 198 |
| | 3 mph | 318 |
| 180 | 2 mph | 204 |
| | 3 mph | 336 |

So if you weigh 160 pounds and walk just one hour per week at 3 mph (and all other activities remain constant), you could burn nearly 5 pounds in one year. The equation is: 318 calories x 52 weeks = 16,536 calories divided by 3,500 (number of calories per pound) = 4.7 pounds.

## The Grr-eat Outdoors

From the backyard to the back woods, the outdoors offers oodles of opportunities for you to play with your dog. Here are some of my all-time favorite activities:

*A simple game of fetch is a good workout for both human and canine.*

**Backyard ball.** This is a good exercise for dogs in a limited space such as a fenced backyard. Engaging in a game of catch helps satisfy your dog's natural instinct to chase and retrieve "prey." If you're not blessed with a major league throwing arm, or your if shoulder gets tired before your fetch-happy dog does, use a tennis racket or rubber tubing to launch the ball.

**Teamwork tug-of-war.** This game burns energy and provides a great exercise outlet for both of you. But be careful. Nip any signs of possible aggression or dominance issues in your dog by clearly establishing the ground rules from the start. Rule #1: You—and only you—should initiate the game of tug. Rule #2: Your dog should release the toy on your command. If his teeth touch your hand, even accidentally, yell "ouch" in a high-pitched voice. End the game immediately, and put the tug toy away.

**Tag, you're it!** Convert this child's game into a fun training exercise for your dog. Start the game with your dog on a leash, in an enclosed room, or in a fenced-in yard. Yell "Tag, you're it" and run away from your dog. Then kneel down. Heap on the praise when your dog bounds after you and sits or lies down in front of you. Repeat a few times until your dog gets the hang of it. This game may come in handy if your dog should get loose. Rather than chase after him, you can yell "Tag, you're it" and sprint the opposite direction to entice him to stop and go toward you.

**On the run.** Jogging offers a quick and easy way to burn calories. Alisa Bauman of Emmaus, Pennsylvania, and a contributing editor for *Runner's World*, frequently jogs with Rhodes, her red Doberman, and offers the following first-hand advice:

- Warm up and cool down with a walk. Start s-l-o-w-l-y. Recognize that it takes time for the two of you to get into a running rhythm and to build endurance.

- Always carry a baggie with you to scoop your dog's "deposits," bring water, and outfit your dog with a bright, reflective vest to make him visible to motorists. Use a leather leash. It is easier to hold and won't cut your hand like a nylon leash will if your dog suddenly decides to dart or lunge. Once your dog consistently matches you stride for stride, you may try a hands-free leash that fits around your waist.

- Choose your routes carefully. Start out on grass so your dog's paws won't get hurt on pavement. Avoid sidewalks that sizzle in the summer or are ice-laden with salt in the winter. Always check your dog's pads for any cuts or injuries. Look for signs of dehydration or overheating in your dog (a slower pace, excessive panting, and dried out tongue). When you stop for water, also give some to your dog.

"It took me quite a while to run well with Rhodes, but now he seems to bond with me during a run," says Bauman. "I even entered him in a local race. We started in the back, but as we started to pick up our pace, all the runners we passed said, 'Oh, cute doggy.'"

*Use an easy-to-grasp object to play fetch in the surf with your dog.*

**Lap it up.** Treat your water-loving dog to a swim. Swimming gives all your dog's muscles a good workout without the jarring impact common with jogging. Select a clean pool or a body of water free of undertows and currents. Before heading to the water, I recommend fitting your dog with a floating device. There are a lot of good doggy life preservers available today in various sizes that will meet your dog's needs.

Some dogs, especially Labradors, love playing fetch in the water. Select a toy that floats and is a size that can be easily mouthed by your dog without risk of swallowing. When swim time is over, always rinse off your dog with warm water and a mild shampoo to reduce his risk of bacterial infections.

**Take a hike.** Take your adventure-seeking dog on a day hike and gradually build his endurance for perhaps a weekend camping trek. Even if you plan only a one-hour hike, always pack a water bottle and a lightweight collapsible water bowl in case your hike goes longer than you anticipate. And honor the first rule of hiking: obey any leash requirements or trail laws.

For longer hikes, always pack a first aid kit, cell phone, water, food, insect repellent, and sunblock. Wear sturdy hiking boots and comfy clothes and consider outfitting your dog with a set of booties to protect his footpads. Make sure your dog sports an ID tag. After a hike, carefully check your dog's body for any ticks, burrs, foxtails, or cuts.

Finally, know the limits of both you and your dog. Short-legged dogs may have trouble navigating some trail conditions or keeping pace with you; short-muzzled dogs are prone to overheating.

## Safety First

Include these items in your first aid kit:

- ✔ ointments (antiseptic creams, rubbing alcohol, hydrogen peroxide, and petroleum jelly)
- ✔ bandages (nonstick sterile gauze pads, cotton balls, swabs, ace bandage, tape)
- ✔ styptic powder
- ✔ cold packs
- ✔ coated buffered aspirin
- ✔ eye wash
- ✔ snakebite kit
- ✔ tools (scissors, tweezers)
- ✔ towels

## Run Solo if Your Dog Is a. . .

Breeds with pushed-in faces have a harder time breathing rapidly than do dogs with normal sized muzzles—especially when temperatures exceed 70° F. These brachycephalic dogs are at risk of collapsing from a run that a Labrador retriever may easily take in stride. Toy breeds also are not natural milers. There are always exceptions, but keep the following breeds on the sidelines while you jog:

Boston terrier
boxer
Brussels griffon
Cavalier King Charles spaniel
Chinese shar-pei
English bulldog
French bulldog
Japanese chin
Lhasa apso
Pekingese
pug
shih tzu
Staffordshire bull terrier

## Skip These Sports

Not all activities are conducive to canines. Topping my list are skateboarding, in-line skating, and road biking, especially if your dog is tagging alongside tethered to the bike. All these activities require maneuvering in and out of traffic, where an unknown hazard may be waiting just around the corner. Even the best-behaved dog can get distracted by something on the route and suddenly dart or abruptly stop. One little mishap between the leash and tire or wheel and you both can go down in a terrible, maybe fatal, heap. Also, no dog can maintain a 15-mph pace, the average speed of a road bike.

One slight exception is mountain biking where the emphasis is not on speed, but on climbing up and down terrain. Some of my friends enjoy outings with their athletic, highly obedient dogs on

*For safety reasons, leave your dog at home if in-line skating is your exercise of choice.*

him know everything is fine. Praise him when he stays by your side and doesn't yank on the leash or stop unexpectedly. Once your dog has demonstrated that he can keep pace next to you, get on your bike and pedal a short distance. Build up the distance slowly as you build up your dog's endurance, confidence, and ability to stay on pace with you.

## Indoor Games— Rain or Shine

Miserable weather shouldn't cancel playtime with your dog. Just move your fun indoors. The advantage of being inside is that your dog is less apt to be distracted (unless you have squirrels scurrying in your living room). Use this uninterrupted time to reinforce basic commands and introduce new tricks.

Dogs don't have a long attention span. Think of them as fidgety elementary school students and spend no more than 5 or 10 minutes at a time teaching each trick. Administer plenty of praise and some healthy food treats to encourage them, and practice, practice, practice so that these tricks become part of your pet's daily routine. Following are a few fun indoor games that also add spice to some basic commands:

wide paths in which they can pedal at a slow, comfortable pace. Their dogs are leashed and jog alongside the bikes.

As with any activity, your dog needs time to acclimate to speed and endurance, especially when jogging next to a bike. When you first start, walk your bike slowly, talking to your dog the whole time to let

**Flip the switch.** Did you forget to turn off the kitchen light and now you're snuggled in bed? Show your dog how to save on utility bills. First, teach him to put his paws on the wall. Pat the wall and say, "up." Now teach him the paw command by pointing at the light switch and pawing it with your hand. Then position him right under the light switch, point to the switch, and say, "paw it." Assist your dog by gently directing his paw to turn the switch off. Praise each success. Eventually, let him go solo without your help. Finally, tap the wall and say, "up, lights out" followed by "paw it, lights out." (For short-legged dogs, place a chair against the wall, tap the seat cushion, and tell your dog, "up.")

**Sing the doggy blues.** Turn your yapping dog into a canine crooner. Play some soulful tunes, toss

*Use command games as an indoor exercise alternative.*

your head back, and unleash a good howl. When your dog joins in, praise him, but keep on howling. Who knows? The two of you may become the next Donny and Marie!

**Flip and catch.** Does your dog constantly hound you for food scraps? Make him work for his treats! Balance a small treat on your dog's nose. Say, "okay" as you glide the treat from your dog's nose to his mouth. Do this several times. Then offer praise only when he tries to flip the treat into his mouth. Finally, balance the treat and the stay command. Take a few steps back, pause, and then say, "okay" for the flip and catch. With each successful snare, lavish praise on your dog.

**I hide, you seek.** Put your dog in a sit, stay position as you hide elsewhere in the house. If necessary, have someone hold your puppy while you hide. Then call your dog by using his name and saying, "come." You may need to repeat his name a few times until he reaches you. Make a big fuss when he finds you. This game reinforces the come command. The purpose behind this game: when you say come, your dog will want to stop whatever he is doing to come to you.

**Doggy jumping jacks.** If your dog adores tennis balls, try this fun game. Tell your dog to sit in front of you. Then hold a tennis ball about a foot directly above his nose. You want to lure him up on his hind feet to sniff and paw for the ball. Keep him on his hind feet for a couple seconds. Then lower the tennis ball to the floor so that he gets back on all four feet. Repeat a few times and finish by tossing the ball for him to fetch.

Add some energetic zip to treat time with these two terrific games offered by professional dog trainer Liz Palika of Oceanside, California. For both games, you will need a handful of dry kibble or a biscuit broken up into small pieces.

**The Come Game.** Put a few pieces of treats in two plastic containers with sturdy lids. You take one container to one end of the living room while a partner takes the second container to the other end of the room. Take turns vigorously rattling the container and calling your dog. When he comes to you, offer him one piece of food. Then have your partner call for your dog and give him a treat when he comes. Have your dog go back and forth until the treats are gone. You are reinforcing the come command.

**The Shell Game.** Take three small bowls of the same size. Sit on the floor and slip a piece of biscuit under one of these upside-down bowls. Tell your dog to find the biscuit and praise him and give him the treat as soon as he finds the correct bowl. Repeat this a few times, but each time move the bowls around so your dog needs to sniff each one to find the tasty treasure.

## A Dog's Dream Toy Box

✔ Kong or a Buster Cube stuffed with food

✔ tug toy

✔ squeaky toy

✔ rip-apart toy

✔ tennis ball

✔ safe chew toy, such as a large, sterilized artificial bone

*Promote games with children and dogs that focus on teamwork, not competition.*

## Don't Forget Kid's Play

Kids and dogs are great partners in play. Playing is important in the development of children and dogs. Dogs can be wonderful teaching tools for children because they give children a sense of safety and a feeling of love. Dogs can help teach empathy, responsibility, and pride to children. Playing in a positive environment can bolster confidence and teach both the benefits of true friendship. It's best to select interactive games for your child and dog that promote teamwork, not competition. My favorites for children six years of age or older are:

**Fetch.** Have your child toss the toy and yell, "fetch." Your child should then kneel down and tell your dog to drop it when he brings the toy back. Instruct your child never to grab the toy out of the dog's mouth. If the dog won't drop the toy, throw a second toy. Often the dog will drop the first toy to pursue the second. Your child should praise the dog each time he fetches the toy and drops it so he learns the rules of the game.

**Where's Sally?** With your dog on a leash in the living room, tell your child to hide in a bedroom. Ask your dog to find your child by saying, "Where's Sally? Find Sally." Guide your dog slowly toward the bedroom and have your child make a noise to attract your dog's attention. When he finds your child, offer praise. Gradually progress until your dog can find the child in the house without being leashed. This game helps reinforce the identities of everyone in the family.

**Beat the clock.** Get your dog into the play mode by attaching the leash to his collar and telling your child to say in an excited voice, "Okay, playtime!" Have your child jump up and down to get your dog happy and interested. Then in the middle of this fun folly, have your child give him a sit or stay command, and tell your child to remain silent. The second your dog obeys, instruct your child to shout praise. Instantly restart this highly animated game. In time, your dog will learn to respond to your child's commands—even during times of excitement or distraction.

**Find it.** This game is ideal for the dog who goes gaga for tennis balls or squeaky toys. Give your dog the sit command and stand a few feet in front of him. Show him his favorite toy then have your child hide it nearby. Now say, "Where's the toy? Find it." When the dog goes to the toy, praise him and offer a small food treat. Gradually have your child place the toy in less visible places, such as in different rooms.

### Success Story: Stephanie Huber and Alfred

When Stephanie Huber wants to tone her biceps and triceps, she doesn't reach for 5-pound free weights; she reaches for Alfred, her accommodating 9-pound Yorkshire terrier.

Huber, a professional dog trainer from Mesquite, Nevada, lies flat on her back on the floor and calls for Alfred. He trots over and she begins her repetitions. Huber hoists Alfred slowly up in the air as she exhales and back down to her chest as she inhales. "I try to do 20 reps, and the whole time he is loving it because he is getting 100 percent of my attention," says Huber. "He's not getting a lot of exercise, but I am. I don't have to worry about flabby arms with Alfred around."

# CHAPTER 7

* * * * * * * * *

# BE A SPORT—TEAM UP WITH YOUR DOG

* * * * * * * * *

On most weekends, from Boston to San Diego, you can find dogs leaping for Frisbees, dancing the cha-cha, and ushering cattle—all in the name of sports. For example, in Los Alamitos, California, stubby-legged dachshunds compete in 50-yard dashes to raise money for local animal shelters. In Chicago, teams of leaping Labradors lunge for tennis balls in timed relay events. In Coltsneck, New Jersey, purebred borzois make hairpin turns at full stride to catch a plastic lure that's just out of reach.

Today's dogs hone their athletic skills and reengage their innate abilities through soaring, fetching, racing, and dancing. They leap off couches into dozens of contests. The sports arena, once the domain of purebreds and AKC-sanctioned events, now welcomes dogs of all sizes, shapes, ages, and physical traits. Mixed-breeds mingle with pedigrees in Frisbee and flyball. Gray-muzzled tail-waggers prove you can teach old dogs new tricks—or at least new dance steps—in canine musical freestyle, which is quickly growing in popularity.

The payoffs for training in agility, Frisbee, canine musical freestyle, flyball, and other canine performance sports go far beyond the chance for blue ribbons, shiny trophies, or titles. While dogs have their day in the ever-expanding sporting world, people discover the fun and thrill of teaming up with their canine companions.

People and dogs are pack animals, and the three most important activities pack animals do together are eat, sleep, and play, says Larry Lachman, Psy.D., a Carmel, California, animal behaviorist and coauthor of *Dogs on the Couch* (Overlook Press, 1999). He says that engaging in deep fun reduces stress for both people and dogs and certainly strengthens the human-animal companion bond. I agree.

Many of today's canine sports promote companionship and collaboration above competition. "Part of the fun of flyball competition is not just the racing but the camaraderie among dogs and people on the same relay teams," says Bob Long of San Diego, tournament director of the North American Flyball Association. "And some of our top teams take pride in the fact that a high percentage of their dogs were rescues from animal shelters."

Indeed, organized sports give dogs an outlet for pent-up energy and an opportunity to develop social skills. Playing sports in a fun and entertaining manner creates a dog with better concentration and behavioral skills. Sports serve as healthy outlets for dogs to use their minds and their muscles, reducing the chance of behavior problems sparked by boredom or inactivity. And both the person and the dog can benefit from aerobic exercise. Calorie-burning activities help you both tone your muscles and improve your stamina so that you will be in better physical shape. Before jumping into an

*Organized sports are beneficial to dogs of all shapes and sizes.*

organized sport with your dog, consider her health and obedience limitations. Your dog may be athletic, but even the top jock dogs are far from invincible. Just like us, canine competitors can be prone to injuries due to improper or inadequate training.

Age, weight, physical stature, and breed all play factors in how well your dog will leap over hurdles, soar airborne to fetch a Frisbee, or bullet through a flyball competition. Keeping your dog fit and healthy should remain your top goal, says M. Christine Zink, D.V.M., Ph.D., from Baltimore, Maryland, an expert in canine sports medicine who has trained dogs in a variety of sports. Before introducing your dog to any performance sport, Dr. Zink recommends that you book an appointment with your veterinarian so that your dog can receive a thorough physical exam. Your veterinarian may discover that your dog has some limiting physical condition such as hip or elbow dysplasia or that she may need to lose a few extra pounds before attempting the rigors of an agility obstacle course.

Athleticism requires more than pure physical prowess; it also depends on mental focus and obedience. A dog learns through the consequences of her behaviors and actions. When a dog does what an owner wants, she gets praised and rewarded. When a dog does something that displeases an owner—such as bolting outside before a leash has been snapped onto her collar—she doesn't collect any rewards. So before a canine athlete can clear a hurdle, snag a Frisbee in midair, or dance the cha-cha in time to music, she must master basic obedience commands. She should be able to sit, stay, and lie down on command and, most importantly, come when called by her owner.

You need to feel confident that your dog will come to you each and every time you call her by name, no matter where you are or what the distractions may be. Identify those distractions—people, toys, food, smells, places, or situations—that steer your dog's attention away from you. Spend a week desensitizing your dog to these distractions by devoting three five-minute sessions each day to practicing recall commands with your dog. Aim for 15 to 25 recalls in a quiet place with no distractions during each session. Once you are successful, introduce distractions during the training to ensure that your dog stays focused on you and your commands.

Once your dog is mentally and physically ready, you may choose to sample a few different sports before settling on one. Let's look in greater detail at some popular dog performance sports and shine a spotlight on some of the top people-dog duos.

## Get an Edge in Agility

**What it is:** Once the domain of Border collies and shelties, agility now attracts dogs of all shapes, sizes, and breeds from surprisingly quick-turning Pomeranians to power-pushing keeshonds. In agility, an owner leads his dog through a fast-paced, timed obstacle course featuring tires, hurdles, chutes, and poles, with the fewest faults possible. Dogs compete in height classes. Common faults include failure to jump over a hurdle, scoot through a tunnel, or touch a contact mark on a platform.

*Agility competitions promote teamwork with animals and humans.*

Owners may not touch their dogs during the race but can otherwise guide them through the course. The winning dog finishes the course in the fastest time with the fewest number of faults.

**Participants:** The United States Dog Agility Association, Inc. (USDAA), the world's largest agility organization, welcomes all dogs regardless of pedigree or size. AKC participants must be registered breeds and at least one year old.

**Gear:** To make inexpensive practice courses, use PVC piping, plywood, barrels, tires, and a children's play tunnel.

**Tips:** Never take your eyes off your dog and use your dog's name to get her attention or to turn her on the agility course. Always tell your dog where to go before you tell her what to do.

**Contacts:**

● **USDAA**
   Telephone: (972) 231-9700
   Web site: www.usdaa.com
   E-mail: info@usdaa.com

● **AKC Agility**
   Telephone: (919) 233-9767
   Web site: www.akc.org

● **The Dog Agility Page**
   Web site: www.dogpatch.org/agility.html

## Agility Profile: Daneen Fox and Chopper

Amid the dozens of Border collies, Australian shepherds, and Jack Russell terriers dominating a recent USDAA competition in Irwindale, California, Chopper, a lap-lounging Pomeranian, looked out of place. But don't be fooled by this idle appearance. Mere moments earlier, Chopper had relied on his 12 pounds of nimble motion to cruise through an obstacle course. Not bad for a dog who didn't take his first agility lesson until age five—proof that you can teach an adult dog a new activity. Now at age seven, he is practically a pro.

Chopper, according to his owner, Daneen Fox of Northridge, California, thrives when it comes to scooting through tunnels and chutes, running all out, and jumping. He is still honing his weave pole skills. She introduced agility to Chopper as a positive outlet for his bottled up energy and constant barking. "I realized he was bored and restless and needed to exercise," says Fox. "We still have a lot to learn about agility, but we'll continue doing this as long as he wants to do it."

### Get Airborne with Frisbee Feats

**What it is:** A catch-and-retrieve sport in which a dog and one thrower attempt to make as many successful throws and catches as possible before time runs out. They earn points based on the difficulty of the catch and the distance of the throw. The sport is played on a rectangular field with lines marked to indicate distances; rounds usually last 1 minute. Advanced competitions, called freestyle, feature timed routines choreographed to music that involve tricks such as a dog leaping off the back of the thrower or doing a half-flip while catching a disc.

**Participants:** Dogs of all breeds and ages who like to chase, leap, catch, and retrieve

**Gear:** Flying discs made of soft plastic

**Tips:** Keep a supply of discs on hand and replace any with sharp edges to avoid harming your dog's teeth or gums. To avoid exhaustion and boredom, always stop practicing while your dog still wants to play.

**Contacts:**

- **Skyhoundz Hyperflite Canine Disc World Championship**
  Telephone: (404) 350-9343
  Web site: www.skyhoundz.com
  E-mail: info@skyhoundz.com
- **International Disc Dog Handlers' Association**
  Web site: www.iddha.com
  E-mail: IDDHA@aol.com

*Outdoor sports like Frisbee help dogs become socialized.*

## Frisbee Sport Profile: Ping Latvong and Nasty Sassy

Nasty Sassy, as her name implies, treats flying discs rudely. She destroys up to 15 of these soaring plastic discs each week. How she destroys them earns her praise and affection from her owner, Ping Latvong of Anaheim, California.

When Latvong slings a disc 30 yards across a grassy park, the five-year-old Border collie stylishly and swiftly pursues it, snatching it in midair. Sometimes she springboards 7 feet into the air off Latvong's chest and makes a bite-down catch. Other times she does 360-degree flips at full stride yards away and lands with the snared disc in her mouth. This human-dog tandem harmonizes supremely well, having finished second twice in the Skyhoundz Hyperflite Canine Disc World Championship.

Latvong and Nasty Sassy travel throughout the country giving Frisbee demonstrations. "Both of us need to be in top physical and mental shape and work fluidly as a team," says Latvong, a hair stylist and bodybuilder. "Sassy is super smart, very intense, and very athletic. She has a lot of energy and picked up the sport right off the bat." Still, Latvong keeps the competition of the sport in perspective. "This sport is all about having fun with your dog," he says. "If we don't win, there's always another day at the park. And believe me, Sassy and I always have fun at the park."

## Get in Step with Canine Musical Freestyle

**What it is:** Freestyle features choreographed musical programs performed by person/dog teams. Each off-leash movement is accomplished by the subtle use of verbal cues and body language.

Scoring is based on a scale of 100, with points awarded for technical and artistic skill. The emphasis is on creativity and communication. Performances range from 90 seconds to 4 minutes based on skill level. There are two canine freestyle organizations listed below.

**Participants:** Dogs of all ages and breeds

**Gear:** Stereo and a wide selection of music

**Tips:** Select music that you enjoy and that perks up your dog because you will be playing the same song repeatedly during rehearsals and performances. Have fun! Start with the basics, including teaching your dog to walk on her hind legs and to step forward and backward in a straight line in response to your hand commands.

**Contacts:**

- **World Canine Freestyle Organization**
  Telephone: (718) 332-5238
  Web site: www.worldcaninefreestyle.org
  E-mail: wcfodogs@aol.com

- **Canine Freestyle Federation, Inc.**
  Telephone: (703) 323-7216
  Web site: www.canine-freestyle.org
  E-mail: president@canine-freestyle.org

## Canine Musical Freestyle Profile: Susan Brogan and Comet

Fred Astaire and Ginger Rogers they're not. But when Susan Brogan and her dog, Comet, hit the dance floor, they bask in applause. "It started as a lark a few years ago," says Brogan, a computer technician from Nokesville, Virginia. "One day I was playing some big band music. Comet perked up and got excited by the music."

Eleven-year-old Comet is full Pembroke Welsh corgi and part ham. In front of audiences, she loves to bark while backing up and rolling over. She weaves through Brogan's legs, flops flat on the floor, and remains motionless for a few seconds—all in sync with the music. Brogan and Comet, who perform in regional competitions and demonstrations at local hospitals and community centers, don matching plaid bow ties as their costumes. Brogan wears a black jacket and tan pants to match Comet's black-and-tan coat. With a fake mustache and brown wooden cane, Brogan hobbles about the dance floor like Charlie Chaplin.

"Comet was an average dog in obedience class, never very technically correct," Brogan said. "But when I put on the music and start twirling my cane, she's in doggy heaven."

## Chase and Race with Flyball

**What it is:** Flyball is a relay race among four-dog teams. When the green light goes on at the starting line, the first dog on each team races down the team's designated 51-foot lane, jumping four hurdles ranging in height from 8 to 16 inches, depending on the smallest dog on the team. At the end of each lane, a machine launches a tennis ball that the dog must catch in midair and return to the starting point, once again clearing all four hurdles. Then the next dog hits the course until all four dogs have run. The winning team completes the course in the fastest time.

**Participants:** All dogs regardless of size or breed. Short, swift dogs rule because hurdle heights are based on the size of the shortest dog in the relay team.

**Gear:** Jumps, flyball boxes (to launch the balls) and tennis balls

**Tips:** Dogs require 6–12 weeks of training; owners need up to six months of classes to learn how to give commands, work on the timing, and master handling dogs in this off-leash sport. Break down each step of the sport and use positive rewards (praise and treats) until your dog has mastered the entire sequence.

*Short dogs excel at flyball.*

**Contact:**

- **North American Flyball Association (NAFA)**
  Telephone: (309) 688-4915
  Web site: www.flyballdogs.com

## Get in Line with Herding Cattle and Sheep

**What it is:** The sport of herding promotes and preserves the inherited herding instinct of certain breeds in sanctioned trials involving various livestock (cattle, sheep, and ducks). Dogs must follow owners' commands to herd animals from pens, guide them through obstacles, and return them to pens.

**Participants:** AKC-registered herding breeds, including Australian shepherds and Border collies

**Gear:** Fenced-in pen, whistle, and livestock

**Tips:** High-scoring dogs can move livestock effectively without a lot of force. You don't need to talk much, but you must position yourself where your dog can see you and the livestock at all times.

**Contacts:**

- **Australian Shepherd Club of America, Inc.**
  Telephone: (409) 778-1082
  Web site: www.asca.org
  E-mail: education@asca.org
- **American Kennel Club**
  Telephone: (919) 233-9767
  Web site: www.akc.org
  E-mail: herding@akc.org
- **United States Border Collie**
  **Handlers Association**

Telephone: (254) 486-2500
Web site: www.usbcha.com

- **American Herding Breed Association**
  Telephone: (508) 761-4078
  Web site: www.ahba-herding.org

### Herding Profile: John Harvey and Apache

Some days, John Harvey swears that his Border collie, Apache, can actually read his thoughts. Mind reading would help with the maintenance of a 6,500-acre cattle and sheep ranch in Simi Valley, California, north of Los Angeles. Often, a herd of 70 or more cattle or sheep stands between Harvey and Apache. "Some days, we can be out eight to ten hours and cover over 20 miles of terrain," says Harvey, a rancher and licensed herding judge for the AKC and American Herding Breed Association. "Apache seems to read my mind. There are about 30 commands for herding, and Apache knows every one of them."

Harvey barely needs to speak, "go by" (steer the herd to the left) or, "bring them" (steer the herd toward him), but Apache follows every audible and cue, zipping back and forth to keep the herd in a tight, moving circle. Eight-year-old Apache's work skills translate into championships: he is the only dog to win first place in both sheep and cattle divisions in the same year (1998) at the Ventura County Fair competition, and he's a three-time county cattle champ.

"What makes Apache exceptional is that he can read the stock and knows how much pressure to apply to keep them moving smoothly in the right direction," Harvey says. "I've been offered $8,000 for Apache, but I'd never sell him. He has the biggest heart and gives everything he's got. He amazes me all the time."

## Get Hooked on Lure Coursing

**What it is:** This sport imitates hare chasing or other games that use artificial lures such as a kitchen garbage bag or plastic bottles. The artificial quarry is attached to a long line strung around a series of pulleys and moves quickly across a large field. The pulleys simulate the course of a zigzagging hare and are controlled by a lure operator. Judges score dogs for their ability to run straightaways, make hairpin turns, quick stops and starts, and closely follow the elusive lure. Most courses are played on 5-acre fields year-round in all but extreme weather conditions. Points are awarded based on a dog's speed, agility, endurance, enthusiasm, and following ability.

**Participants:** Limited to AKC-registered purebreds, including Afghan hound, basenji, borzoi, greyhound, Ibiza hound, Irish wolfhound, pharaoh hound, Rhodesian Ridgeback, saluki, Scottish deerhound and whippet

**Gear:** A series of pulleys, a plastic lure, and a long string or fishing line

**Tips:** Lure coursing appeals mostly to hunting breeds because of their chase instinct. Start training your puppy by fastening a lure to the end of a string in the house and encouraging her to give chase. Let your dog see a few lure-coursing events before enrolling her in a lure-coursing training program.

**Contacts:**

● **American Sighthound Field Association**
  Telephone: (904) 682-2272
  Web site: www.asfa.org

### Lure Coursing Profile: Bonnie Dalzell and her dogs

Bonnie Dalzell has bred, trained, and handled champion borzois, earning more lure-coursing championship titles than anyone else—she has trained more than 110 titled dogs. She also maintains a Web site to promote the sport to newcomers.

Dalzell witnessed her first lure-coursing event in 1977, in Berkeley, California. Watching hounds pursue lures reinforced her belief that these dogs needed an organized sport that catered to their instinctive desire to chase prey. "Back then, there was no agility or flyball," says Dalzell, a kennel owner in Hydes, Maryland. "Your choices in sports for dogs were quite limited." She continues, "My first coursing dog was Darkness, who was so fabulous that we finally stopped coursing her to allow others to start winning. She had three litters—11 puppies total—and of them, 6 earned titles. Her legacy continues."

A former anatomy professor at a veterinary university, Dalzell pays close attention to her dogs' growing physiques, looking for anomalies in their spines and testing their range of flexibility before allowing them to compete. "Lure coursing is a demanding sport, and it's important to make sure your dogs are in good physical shape to prevent injuries," she says. "Something as simple as regular nail trimming and examining the webbing of the toes for signs of thorns, splinters, or cuts shouldn't be overlooked. Dogs run at speeds of 35 mph on a lure course, and the condition of their feet is very important."

- **American Kennel Club**

  Telephone: (919) 233-9767

  Web site: www.akc.org

  E-mail: coursing@akc.org

## Get a Feel for Field Trials

**What it is:** Field trials are a head-to-head test of over-all hunting agility with groupings by breed. The competition replicates actual hunting situations. Dogs retrieve real birds launched into the meadow or field while ignoring decoy birds and other distractions. Trials call for one dog to be active in the field while the others remain at the starting line completely still, next to their owners. Each dog starts with a perfect score of zero and gains points for infractions. The dog with the lowest score wins. Classes are based on ability, not age.

**Participants:** Open to AKC-registered beagles, pointing breeds, retrievers, spaniels, basset hounds, and dachshunds

**Gear:** Decoys and hunting equipment such as guns, camouflage clothing, and boots

**Tips:** Keep your dog within control distance and obedient to your commands while in the field. Build up her endurance gradually so she will be able to compete at full speed and strength. At a young age, introduce your dog to guns, boats, decoys, and any equipment she might encounter in the field.

**Contacts:**

- **American Kennel Club**

  Telephone: (919) 233-9767

  Web site: www.akc.org

  E-mail: fieldtrials@akc.org

- **North American Hunting Retriever Association**

  Telephone: (540) 286-0625

  Web site: www.nahra.org

  E-mail: nahra@juno.com

### Success Story: Wendy Pope and Tasha, Loki, and Ben-Shiva

A few years ago, Wendy Pope was pencil pushing as a financial analyst in downtown Toronto, Canada. Today, she pushes up hills and mountains in picturesque British Columbia with her two German shepherds, Tasha and Loki, and her husky mix, Ben-Shiva. For them, a routine hike is two hours minimum at elevations that are often 9,000 feet or higher. The joys and benefits of working out together are undeniable. "I traded my career in finance to open a fitness spa in Ainsworth Hot Springs," says Pope, a fit 52-year-old. "It's heaven here and it's healthful exercise for all of us. My dogs are happy and in great shape and so am I."

# CHAPTER 8

\* \* \* \* \* \* \* \* \* \*

# MIND OVER
# WEIGHTY MATTERS

\* \* \* \* \* \* \* \* \* \*

How strong is your willpower? Can you say no to chocolate? What's the average shelf life of cookies in your house—weeks, days, or hours? Never underestimate the psychological powers of food—especially those that are sweet, fried, and loaded with calories. Mindless eating or eating out of boredom, sadness, depression, or anxiety not only fills us up, but fills us out as well. And, too often, many of us extend this attitude of misery loves food to our ready-to-please canine pals. Then together we wolf down too much of the wrong food.

My dad, Tom, was a lifelong fan of dogs, but instead of taking a walk with his pal, he would "invite" Keesha, his ever-smiling keeshond, to join him for a mid-afternoon car ride to a fast-food restaurant. Dad would pull up to the drive-thru window and order two mega-burgers and supersized french fries. He and Keesha would gulp down their fatty feasts in less than a minute! My dad battled a host of medical problems all his life, partly due to being overweight, before dying at age 73; Keesha nearly died from pancreatitis at the young age of 7 from their burger-bonding episodes.

Dad heeded his veterinarian's strong advice and stopped feeding fast food to Keesha. Keesha would hop in the car for their fast-food runs but instead of a greasy burger, she received a healthy biscuit from a bag Dad stashed in his glove compartment. The break from burgers essentially saved Keesha's life.

She slimmed down, regained some puppylike vigor, and lived to be 14. Dad, however, didn't have the willpower to stop making those afternoon fast-food runs for his own health. "I know eating this burger is not good for me, but I had no idea it could harm Keesha," my dad told me. "I learned my lesson. But, it's easier to make the right food choices for Keesha than it is for me. I have a tough time saying no to a burger."

Food can be a powerful lure, but there are positive ways to break negative habits. Annie Glasgow of Saint Paul, Minnesota, is a licensed social worker and therapist who helps people of all ages reprogram their mindset. She is also blessed to have shared her life with three golden retrievers: Muffin, Burnout, and Baffin. "They were, and remain in my heart, inspiration," notes Glasgow. "I was forever in awe at the wonder of their intelligence, joy of freedom and exercise, and gift of compassion they gave to me and my family."

Saying no to food takes a lot of psychological fortitude, says Glasgow. It is important to consciously decide if the food we are eating is satisfying our physical needs rather than our mental desires. Turning to food for comfort, an expression of love, or as a solution to such problems as loneliness or unhappiness is merely a diet filled with too many emotional calories that we don't need.

Live your life in the present tense; that's the only place any of us can take any action. If you're impa-

tient and are looking for instant results, you'll become frustrated and the process of trying to maintain a healthy weight will overwhelm you. Remember the magic equation Process = Time = Results.

Glasgow offers these four ways to bolster one's willpower, especially at mealtime:

**1.** Recognize that you are in control and that you are the expert of you.

**2.** Remember that "worry is the interest you pay on trouble before it's due."

**3.** Discover and exercise your sense of humor.

**4.** Make sure that the goals you set are your goals.

## Halt Those Beggin' Eyes

You may have the willpower to resist chocolate cake, but the bigger challenge may be resisting that tail wagging away at your feet. Dogs are masters at projecting hungry eyes—even if their bellies are touching the floor. How can you resist that slight drool and ever-so-subtle whimper, begging for a piece of your burger or a few of your french fries? Very quickly, your dog will recognize that when people gather around the dining room table, lip-smacking goodies are available. If you have trouble saying no, you need some viable solutions. The next time your dog comes

*Have your dog respond to a sit command before providing a treat.*

begging, treat him to a calorie-free hug or an up-and-down-the-back massage instead.

For a long-lasting solution, introduce some table manners. Teach your dog, no matter what age, how to ask politely for food. It starts with your dog recognizing that you are the esteemed Keeper of Chow, a person to be treated with respect.

At mealtime, tell your dog to lie down as you slowly lower his food dish a few inches from the floor. Reward the behavior and gradually lower the bowl closer to the floor with each repetition. If your dog leaps up and lurches for the bowl, lift the dish straight up and wait for him to lie down again. When he does, then lower the dish again. When he stays still until the dish touches the floor, say, "okay" and let him eat. Once your dog masters this stage, work on having him stay for varying lengths of time while the dish is on the floor, even when you turn your back or leave the room. Mastering this exercise will make mealtime far less chaotic—and you will be the one in control.

Another tasteful tactic is to instill in your dog the idea that he must work for his food. Don't freely give food from your plate. Have your dog respond to a sit, stay, or leave it command first before handing over food. And stick with foods that are not high in fat such as lean bits of meat, unbuttered popcorn, or carrots.

During this transition time, when you're converting your ravenous chowhound into a canine connoisseur, consider feeding him in a different room so that you and your family can enjoy an uninterrupt-

ed meal in the dining room. Or put him in his crate with a chew toy stuffed with peanut butter or some other favorite yummy treat to keep him occupied while you eat.

The bottom line: if you keep your dog from begging for table scraps, you can help ensure him a long, happy life.

*Reach for the Frisbee instead of a cookie the next time you have the urge to snack.*

## Play Mind Games—Cuddle Your Canine

One's outlook on life can also contribute to mindless overeating. Monitor your moods and gauge whether you tend to snack more when you're sad, lonely, or feeling celebratory. At times I've convinced myself that I deserve to eat three pieces of carrot cake because I didn't land that dream job or because I did land that dream job and wanted to celebrate. Strive to be more hopeful, calm, and resilient; opt for optimism. National studies indicate that optimists live longer than pessimists. For example, a University of Kentucky researcher received psychology's largest monetary prize for her research showing the health benefits of optimism. Suzanne C. Segerstrom, Ph.D., an assistant professor of psychology at the University of Kentucky, was the first place winner of the 2002 Templeton Positive Psychology Prize. The $100,000 award was divided as a cash prize of $30,000 to be used any way Dr. Segerstrom chooses, and a grant of $70,000 to support her research in the positive psychology field.

For an attitude adjustment, all you have to do is turn to your dog, one of the best mental motivators and inner healers on this planet. Dogs are nature's underrated and overlooked form of Prozac. They have the ability to raise our levels of serotonin, endorphins, and other feel-good body chemicals. In a recent study conducted by researchers at the University of Buffalo School of Medicine and Biomedical Sciences in New York, people with pets, dogs in particular, had a lower blood pressure and heart rate than petless people. Pets are also heralded for their abilities to prevent, detect, treat, and in some cases, cure a variety of mental and physical maladies.

*Even dogs need some time alone.*

To help you stay on the path to good fitness and nutrition, consider these five reasons dogs make great role models:

**1. Dogs act as natural yoga teachers.** Dogs know the value of purposeful stretching to work muscle groups before vacating that warm spot on the bed. Watch your dog to learn some simple yoga stretches you can do before your feet even touch the floor.

**2. Dogs know the therapeutic value of touch.** Dogs aren't shy about asking for hugs and mini-massages. Take a cue and seek out hugs and therapeutic massages from family and friends to unknot those muscle snarls on your neck, shoulders and back.

**3. Dogs know the value of solitude.** Spending some time alone each day is vital to recharging one's batteries. Dogs can have stress, too, and they need some alone time just like humans.

**4. Dogs know the value of power napping.** Your dog uses mininaps throughout the day to recharge and revive. If you could take a 10-minute afternoon nap, you would be in talented company. Many creative people, including inventor Thomas Edison, were power nappers.

**5. Dogs live in the present.** Dogs don't get caught up in the "should haves" and "what ifs" way of thinking that breeds guilt, stress, and worry. Follow your dog's cues by trying to live more in the moment and dealing with actual situations instead of fretting about what might happen.

## Success Story: Jim Minton and Austin

Wearing a police badge since 1999, Austin, a golden Labrador, has located missing children, hikers, Alzheimer's patients, and victims trapped at disaster sites. He has even found key evidence in murder cases as a full-fledged, four-footed member of the Austin, Texas, police department.

To stay in shape, he and his partner, Officer Jim Minton, reach new heights—repelling nearby Enchanted Rock. Minton straps his harness to Austin and the tandem climb up and down the sides of mountains. "It's a great workout and great practice in case we need to repel to find lost hikers," says Minton. "We can be dangling high in the air and I look at Austin and he's grinning. What a dog." Jim and Austin are wonderful examples of how a great positive attitude can garner amazing accomplishments—such as literally climbing a mountain.

# CHAPTER 9

* * * * * * * *

# TROUBLESHOOTING TACTICS

* * * * * * * *

Congratulations! You and your dog are making steady progress on a diet and exercise plan. Both of you have slimmed down and toned up. But watch out—even the most fitness conscious can fall prey to slipups due to holidays, injuries, and sheer boredom. If any—or all—of these scenarios sound familiar, don't feel guilty. Recognize these as temporary setbacks and gear up to get you and your dog back on the healthy track.

## Put a Halt to Holiday Temptations

You've been eating sensibly and exercising with your dog consistently since July. Then Thanksgiving arrives, immediately followed by holiday parties in December. There's gravy-laden turkey and holiday cookies and you find yourself slipping back into bad eating habits, and you're not finding time to work out with your weight-gaining dog. You can survive holidays without gaining an ounce. Repeat that sentence. Out loud. Dan Hamner, M.D., a sports medicine physician and marathon runner in New York City, offers these holiday survival tactics that allow you to indulge, celebrate, and stay slim:

1. Park at the remote end of the shopping mall, which forces you to walk to the stores. Make frequent trips to your car to unload your purchases.

2. Politely say no to free samples. A cracker with one ounce of port wine totals 110 calories and nearly 8 g of fat; one piece of fudge totals 80 calories and 3 g of fat. Little by little, these nibblers can add up to plenty of calories and fat grams.

3. Skip the cinnamon bun stores and cookie shops. Instead, pack a chocolate energy bar that typically averages only 250 calories and offers you a bonus 5 g of fiber.

4. Squeeze in 10-minute mini workout sessions by dancing to holiday songs or having your dog join you in a jog up and down the stairs three times.

5. Save on calories by drinking a wine spritzer (80 calories, 0 g of fat) instead of a rum toddy (330 calories and 11 g of fat).

As for your dog, stick with her regular diet. Treats of turkey, ham, gravy, cookies, or other goodies can cause gastrointestinal upset in your dog because she is not accustomed to eating these holiday delights. Also, ask your guests not to fall prey to your dog's begging behavior by feeding her people food.

Keep in mind that holidays create disruptions in household routines and that your dog craves routine. You will be pressed for time during the holidays, but stick to your daily exercise rituals with your dog, albeit, in shorter durations. This will keep her content and calm amid all the holiday frenzy, help her unleash her pent-up energy, and help you both keep off the pounds.

*Avoid giving dogs holiday treats like candy and cookies.*

## Time-Out for Injuries

You take a spill and break your wrist. In the same week, your dog trips and sprains her back leg. You throb; she limps. Mutually, you agree to temporarily shelve your post-dinner walks together. You feel the pounds returning.

Accidents and injuries can occur at any time to anyone or to any active dog. If this happens to your dog, always work closely with your veterinarian to assist in your dog's recovery. And practice patience.

Soft tissue injuries and broken limbs take time to mend. Recognize the small steps needed for improvement, and remind yourself that the two of you will soon be back in fit form.

The acronym RICE (rest, ice, compression, and elevation) applies to both two-legged and four-legged athletes nursing muscle injuries. Again, first consult your physician or your dog's veterinarian for medical advice. In general, apply ice on acute injuries during the first 48 hours. Ice offers pain

*Stretch first to avoid injury later.*

relief and constricts blood vessels to minimize swelling. Apply the ice for 20 minutes every few hours during this two-day period following an injury. If you're applying ice to a dog's injury, pay attention to her cues and remove the ice pack if she appears uncomfortable.

Follow the ice treatments with heat to enhance blood flow. Heat therapy can speed healing, reduce lactic acid buildup, and tame muscle spasms. Warm a moist towel in the microwave or apply a heat gel pack or heating pad to the injured area.

If your dog likes water, treat mending muscles with hydrotherapy. You can take a garden hose and run water over the sore site (do not use a high-pressure nozzle gun) or fill the bathtub and let your dog soak for 10–15 minutes. If you have a whirlpool attachment, let the rushing waters work their magic on your dog. Slowly wading into a lake, stream, or pool and using gentle swimming strokes can also help restore muscle strength and endurance without taxing joints.

*Choose natural surfaces for running to lessen stress on joints.*

Lessen the risk of injury for both you and your dog by stretching before every activity and paying attention to your physical limitations. For example, avoid introducing your growing puppy to sports too soon. Growth plates in dogs do not fully form until 12–18 months of age, depending on the breed. In agility, for instance, young dogs should only jump hurdles that are a few inches high until the dogs

reach physical maturity; adhering to this guideline reduces the risk of bone or muscle tears and breaks.

On the other end of the age spectrum, respect your elders—senior dogs and people, that is. During your daily walks, seek routes with grass or dirt rather than concrete sidewalks, which can add stress to joints with each stride. This is especially important for arthritic dogs and people. Learn how to gently massage your dog to improve blood flow, circulation, and to ease muscle stiffness. Pet- and people-proof your house by wiping up spills from water bowls or sinks to prevent slipping.

Install a safety gate across stairways so that stiff-moving dogs do not try to climb down the stairs and take a tumble.

For dogs and people of all ages, sidestep the weekend warrior mentality. Resist the temptation to turn your dog into a Saturday-Sunday jock and a weekday sofa lounger. Dogs who are not consistently exercised run the risk of pulling muscles or lacking the stamina to complete a sports event such as an agility course. During the week, incorporate short sprints during your daily walks to build up stamina for both of you.

## Turn Ho-Hum into Hooray!

Ho-hum. You feel yourself yawning as you and your dog prepare to go on the same 45-minute route that you've taken everyday for the past six months. Even she seems bored passing the same scenery. Both of you plod along, counting the strides, until you're back home and on the sofa. Beware of boredom! Dogs may crave routine but they detest repetition. A lot of destructive canine behavior is due to a dog who is bored or one who receives inadequate exercise.

Attitude is everything to a dog, who looks to you for guidance. If you speak in a monotone and use few gestures when playing with your dog, she will soon regard learning a new trick or snagging a tossed tennis ball as a chore or a big bore. Get animated. Praise, praise, praise. Let your dog see that you're having a grand time.

*Trade in a routine walk for playtime at the dog park to add variety.*

To keep both you and your dog upbeat, vary your walk routes, times, and distances. Use your walk time to reinforce such commands as heel, sit, and roll over, or to teach a new trick that will wow your neighbors. Treat your adult dog to a romp at a dog park—the canine version of a social after-work dance. Your dog gets to be a dog, hang around other dogs, play tag, chase, and playfully wrestle. However, don't regard a dog park as a place to drop off your dog while you go shopping. Dog parks are like a child's playground; you need to be there to supervise the play and to step in at the first sign of any problems.

Follow these other dog park pointers to ensure a fun outing:

- Leave your dog's favorite toy at home. She may not like the notion of having to share it with a slobbering Great Dane.
- Call your dog to you periodically and reward her with food treats so that she still views you as top dog.
- Be your dog's personal pooperscooper and clean up her deposits.

Spice up the daily routine with an occasional indulgence. For you, book an afternoon of pampering at a day spa or take the afternoon off

*Indulge yourself occasionally with a favorite activity, like reading a book.*

from work to play a round of golf or read a favorite book. For your dog, treat her to a visit to a doggy day care center where she can romp with other four-legged friends.

The ultimate boredom-buster is booking a vacation and taking your dog. These days, the Dogs Welcome mat is appearing more frequently at inns, parks, and other places. Check the Internet for many resources that provide details on fun-filled dog getaways. A couple of helpful sites are www.dogfriendly.com and www.dogscouts.com, which is the Web site of one of my favorite doggy vacation spots. Dog Scouts of America is a camp in Michigan run by professional dog trainer Lonnie Olson. At Dog Scouts of America, canine attendees can earn merit badges during their stay.

---

## Doggy Day Care Checklist

What makes a doggy day care center a good match for your dog? Here are some tips:

1. **Preview the place before you enroll your dog.** On the first visit, leave your dog at home so that you can focus on what the center offers. Watch how dogs interact with each other and with people; notice how dogs are treated.

2. **Look, listen, and sniff.** The center should be clean, free of doggy odors, and filled with happy dog talk, not whines and aggressive growls. Urine and fecal matter should be quickly cleaned with disinfectants.

3. **Check the climate.** Is the center air-conditioned and well ventilated? Are there ample safe places for dogs to get some outdoor exercise, too?

4. **Look at the layout.** Are big dogs separated from tiny ones? Are there safe toys inside these areas? Are there places for dogs to nap?

5. **Ask about introductions.** How is a new dog introduced to the pack of regulars? Some places like to have a staff member shadow the new dog for a day or two to ease her acceptance by the other dogs. Make sure the center does temperament tests on dogs and properly segregates highly submissive or fearful dogs from highly confident, dominant dogs. Centers usually provide written rules, including the right to expel dogs exhibiting aggressive behavior, to protect the safety of the other dogs.

6. **Consider the staff.** Ideally, the ratio of dogs per staff member should not exceed 10:1. Do the staffers rely on positive reinforcement techniques rather than physical punishment?

7. **Do a health check.** Reputable centers require clients to show proof that their dogs receive regular flea and tick treatments, are current on their vaccinations, and are not aggressive to other dogs or people.

8. **Gauge the personal level of attention.** Are your dog's personal supplies (food, medications, leashes) kept in a separate container? Does the staff greet dogs by their names and recognize their special dietary needs and personality traits?

9. **Scout the center for safety.** Are there double doors preventing dogs from escaping or fleeing into the streets? Are medications and cleaning chemicals stored out of paw's reach? Is there a safe confined outdoor area for dogs or do handlers make sure dogs are walked on leashes? Does the staff insist that all dogs wear ID tags?

10. **Do a trial run.** Schedule your dog to spend one day at the center. When you come to pick her up at the end of the day, notice how your dog behaves. Does she seem happy and relaxed—or anxious and tense? Does she happily go up to members of the staff or cower and back away from them?

# Yippee! It's a Snow Day!

Remember how jazzed you got as a child when your school closed due to snow? You couldn't wait to race outside to make a snow angel. No need for you and your dog to suffer through cabin fever during the cold winter days.

Let your dog adjust to the colder temperatures by slowly extending her time outdoors. And factor in the windchill, which can make the outdoor air feel considerably colder than is indicated on the thermometer. Consider donning your thin-coated dog in a sweater-vest to help insulate him against the cold. If you want to put booties on your dog's feet, be sure they fit snugly but not tight enough to cut off circulation in the feet.

Romps in the snow can be fun and energizing. For dogs who love to chase and retrieve, play snowball fetch. For diggers and scent-minded dogs such as terriers and beagles, play "hide-the-biscuit-in-the-snowbank." Just remember that the longer a dog stays outside during cold weather, the greater her risk for developing hypothermia. By definition, hypothermia is a dangerous drop in the body's core body temperature. Usher your dog inside if you notice any of these warning signs:

✔ prolonged and aggressive shivering

✔ no interest in playing outdoors

✔ weak or lethargic behavior, especially if she is usually a high-energy dog

✔ confusion or disorientation exhibited by walking in circles or not recognizing her name

Once inside, wrap your dog in warm towels or blankets and turn up your thermostat. Stay with your dog until she stops shivering. When her condition improves, feed her food and water to provide added warmth and strength. If your dog's condition worsens, however, or if she becomes unconscious, contact your veterinarian immediately.

Also, watch for any signs of fatigue in your snow-bounding dog and end the snow games when appropriate. Maintain a supply of dry towels by the door and dry your dog each time she comes inside. Pat down her fur and check her footpads for any signs of injury. Prevent static electricity and dry skin on your dog by operating a humidifier to add more moisture to the indoor air. Aim for 25–30 percent humidity inside your home. And keep it humming.

Most outside activities that are safe in warmer temperatures are also safe in the winter as long as there is not an excessive amount of snow and ice or unsafe temperatures.

## Success Story: Susan Kalish and Norton

Susan Kalish, executive director of the American Running Association, has learned to exercise her dog, Norton, the same way she learned to exercise her children: gradually and always with an element of fun.

As a growing pup, Norton, a West Highland terrier, started by walking with Kalish. Slowly, the pair went from walking around the block to walking around two blocks to three and finally, they expanded to a 3-mile loop. Once Norton proved he could go the distance, Kalish started to work on his speed. "At first, we'd run at a slow pace and then walk (and stop to sniff), then run, then walk," says Kalish. "Now, we charge up hills, meander around ponds, and race to Zoe's house (a little girl Norton likes). And sometimes I let him take the lead and now he helps me work on my speed."

# CHAPTER 10

* * * * * * * * * *

# TOP 12 FOOD AND FITNESS MYTHS

* * * * * * * * * *

The moon is made of green cheese. If you swallow watermelon seeds, you will grow a watermelon in your belly. And, no-fat cookies are calorie-free, so eat all you desire. Facts? Far from it. Many groundless claims also exist in the dog world. Allow me to debunk a dozen of the most common incorrect doggone myths:

**Myth #1:** A dog who is spayed or neutered will become overweight.

**Fact:** Contrary to popular belief, spayed and neutered dogs don't automatically balloon into plump pooches after these surgical procedures. In fact, these dogs tend not to need as much food as their intact peers. Since you control the food bowl,

*Provide your dog with healthy food portions along with plenty of toys to increase his activity level.*

watch the amount you serve your dog. Need more good reasons to have your pet altered? On average, they live longer, healthier lives; are less likely to develop certain cancers or to exhibit behavior problems (blame sex hormones for a dog's tendency to roam, mark his territory by urinating in the house, and fight with other dogs). And you'll do your part to control canine overpopulation.

**Myth #2:** As long as I feed my dog the same amount of food every day, he will never gain weight.

**Fact:** How much you need to pour into your dog's food bowl depends on a lot of factors, including age and activity level. You need to pay attention to both. A senior dog needs less food (but more protein) than a growing puppy because his metabolism slows with age. On the other hand, your fast-growing puppy needs more food per day than he will once he is in his prime, especially if he is not very active. By feeding your adult dog the same amount you did when he was a puppy, you risk having him pack on the pounds slowly but steadily over time. No matter the age, high-energy dogs require more food than couch-seeking canines.

**Myth #3:** Feeding my dog once a day will guarantee that he never becomes overweight.

**Fact:** It's actually better to feed your dog two or three small meals per day, rather than one large one since eating burns 10–15 percent of ingested calories. And your chowhound will certainly be pleased to receive two or three meals instead of one. Just make sure that the amount you serve remains constant. By the way, follow the same advice for yourself. Eat five to six small meals a day and don't eat any food a few hours before bedtime to help control your weight.

*Crash dieting is unhealthy for dogs and humans. Instead, control food and increase exercise.*

**Myth #4:** A raw meat diet is nutritionally balanced. Dogs benefit from gnawing on raw bones.

**Fact:** A pure raw meat diet delivers little calcium and fiber and can actually cause serious health problems in your dog. Raw bones expose your dog to possible intestinal parasites or salmonella. Bone splinters can lodge in the throat or rupture stomach lining. Nowadays, premium commercial dog foods are loaded with nutrients, which, bite for bite, can satisfy your dog's nutritional and health needs better than a raw meat diet.

**Myth #5:** The best way to get an obese dog back in shape is to put him on a crash diet.

**Fact:** A dog who is 30 percent overweight should take about six months to reach his ideal weight through reduced food portions. Crash diets can cause more harm than good to your dog. Team up with your veterinarian to gradually cut back on your dog's calories and slowly introduce an exercise program to keep the pounds off permanently.

**Myth #6:** My dog has his own gym—my backyard. He will exercise on his own while I'm at work.

**Fact:** Dogs are social animals who thrive in packs. Even though you may have a fenced backyard complete with canine amenities such as a doghouse, water and food bowls, and toys, your dog's top

*Dogs crave interaction and social contact.*

**Fact:** Dogs who do not receive adequate regular exercise are at risk of being chubby, bored, and mischievous; they may resort to nonstop barking, chewing, or digging. They need an outlet for their energy. Maintain a regular exercise schedule that satisfies the age, health condition, and energy level of your dog. For some low-energy dogs, a 20-minute daily walk may be ample, but raring-to-go dogs may benefit from spending 40 minutes playing and chasing other dogs in a local dog park or joining you in a 2-mile jog or brisk walk. A dog who gets adequate exercise is less destructive and tends to sleep soundly through the night.

**Myth #8:** It's perfectly normal for dogs to get chubby during the winter. After all, you can't exercise your dog during cold weather.

**Fact:** In general, dogs who don't exercise as much in the winter as they do in the summer need less food to maintain their weight. Still, a slight weight gain (5 percent or less) during the winter can provide your dog with added insulation against cold temperatures. Some dogs are thrilled by winter's chill, however, and can't wait to head outdoors. Certain breeds such as huskies, Alaskan malamutes, and Labradors have thick coats designed to withstand cold weather better than thin-coated breeds such as beagles, Jack Russell terriers, and greyhounds. Active dogs can burn more calories during the winter, so check your dog's weight weekly and adjust the food portions accordingly.

desire is to interact with you and others in your household. Dogs serving solitary confinement in backyards are prone to become escape artists, excessive barkers, diligent diggers, or overly excited greeters because they are starved for attention. Spend time with your dog in the backyard tossing a ball or Frisbee or engaging in other activities so that he views the backyard as a fun place to be and not a place of isolation. When you're home, have your dog spend most of his time indoors with you. Crates and see-through gates can be used to confine your dog to a specified area inside the house when necessary.

**Myth #7:** Your dog is deliberately being bad when he digs in your garden, barks incessantly, and chews on your leather loafers.

*Schedule regular rest and water breaks during exercise to avoid overheating.*

**Myth #9:** For a truly effective workout, my muscles should be sore and my dog should be dog-tired.

**Fact:** Don't buy into the no-pain-no-gain attitude. Pace yourselves by getting your bodies used to the physical workout. Slowly add a few minutes a day and gradually increase the intensity to allow your muscles and joints adequate time to get in condition. If you or your dog experiences pain, view it as a red flag that you are overtaxing your muscles and need to cut back.

**Myth #10:** My nine-month-old Border collie is a true jock. The sooner he competes in agility, the more fit he will become.

**Fact:** Don't let your dog's puppy enthusiasm fool you. Be patient. Wait for your dog to reach his first birthday before having him compete in activities that require jumping. Depending on the breed, the growth plates are not fully formed until a dog becomes 12-18 months old, so hold off on agility competition. The sport's jarring movements, quick darts, and high leaps can cause permanent skeletal and muscular damage in still-growing puppies. Temper your impatience by enrolling your dog in a puppy agility class that is taught and carefully supervised by a professional trainer who will take precautions to protect growing muscles and joints.

**Myth #11:** Dogs are natural athletes. They don't need to condition themselves every day.

**Fact:** Resist the temptation to turn your dog into a weekend warrior. Dogs who lounge on a sofa all week lack the conditioning to properly handle the physical demands of running, swimming, or competing in performance sports such as agility on weekends. These only-on-weekend physical demands can cause muscle injuries. Dogs should be exercised at least 20 minutes a day, even if you break that up into two 10-minute brisk walks.

**Myth #12:** Dogs stop playing when they get tired.

**Fact:** In general, dogs aren't quitters, even when they become injured or completely exhausted. Their drive to please people often overpowers common sense. It's up to us to read our dogs' signs of fatigue and step in to give them a well-deserved breather. Stop a physical activity if your dog starts to pant rapidly, shifts his body weight to indicate muscle soreness, or his saliva changes from clear to a white foam.

## Success Story: Ganay Johnson and Elvis

Meet a four-legged Elvis that ain't nothing like a chowhound! Every morning, Ganay Johnson and Elvis, her 12-year-old Labrador mix, enjoy a 3-mile run. They also like to hike and backpack in the summers and cross-country ski in the winters (okay, Elvis tags along without skis). "Even at his age, Elvis really likes to exercise," says Johnson, an executive director for an animal shelter in Bozeman, Montana. "If I get lazy and lay off running for a few days, Elvis protests. He paces in the morning and 'speaks' to me. He keeps me honest—and in shape."

*Dogs should be exercised at least 20 minutes a day.*

# Appendix A

★ ★ ★ ★ ★ ★ ★ ★ ★

# HELPFUL ADDRESSES

★ ★ ★ ★ ★ ★ ★ ★ ★

**American Kennel Club**
5580 Centerview Drive, Suite 200
Raleigh, NC 27505
(919) 233-9767

**American Veterinary Medical Association**
1931 North Meacham Road, Suite 100
Schaumburg, IL 60173
(847) 925-8070

**Animal Behavior Society**
c/o Indiana University
2611 East 10th Street #170
Bloomington IN 47408-2603
(812) 856-5541

**Association of Professional Dog Trainers**
66 Morris Ave., Suite 2-A
Springfield, NJ 07081
(800) PET-DOGS

**Canine Freestyle Federation**
Joan Tennille, President
4207 Minton Drive
Fairfax, VA 22032
(703) 323-7216

**Friskies ALPO Canine Frisbee Disc**
Peter Bloeme
4060-D Peachtree Road, Suite 326
Atlanta, GA 30319
(800) 786-9240

**North American Flyball Association**
1400 W. Devon Ave.
Box 512
Chicago, IL 60660
(309) 688-4915

**United States Dog Agility Association (USDAA)**
P.O. Box 850955
Richardson, TX 75085
(972) 231-9700

**World Canine Freestyle Organization**
Patie Ventre, founder
P.O. Box 350122
Brooklyn, NY 11235
(718) 332-5238

# Appendix B

★ ★ ★ ★ ★ ★ ★ ★ ★

# INTERNET RESOURCES

★ ★ ★ ★ ★ ★ ★ ★ ★

**Canine Nutrition**

| | |
|---|---|
| Hill's Pet Nutrition | www.petfit.com |
| PetDIETS.com | www.petdiets.com |
| Nestlé Purina Pet Care | www.purina.com |
| Nestlé Purina Fit & Trim | www.fitandtrim.com/home.htm |

**Canine Health and Well-Being**

| | |
|---|---|
| American Kennel Club | www.akc.org |
| American Veterinary Medical Association | www.avma.org |
| Animal Behavior Society | www.animalbehavior.org |
| Dog Owner's Guide | www.canismajor.com/dog/alltopic.html |
| Linda Tellington's Ttouch therapy | www.lindatellingtonjones.com |
| PetEducation.com | www.peteducation.com |
| Supplement Quality | www.supplementquality.com |

**Activities and Training**

| | |
|---|---|
| Association of Professional Dog Trainers | www.apdt.com |
| Canine Freestyle Federation | www.canine-freestyle.org |
| Dog Play | www.dog-play.com |
| Friskies Alpo Canine Frisbee Disc | www.skyhoundz.com |
| International Disc Dog Handlers Association | www.iddha.com |
| North American Flyball Association | http://muskie.fishnet.com/~flyball |
| United States Dog Agility Association | www.usdaa.com |
| World Canine Freestyle Organization | www.woofs.org |

# RESOURCE BOOKS

Ackerman, Lowell, D.V.M. *Canine Nutrition: What Every Owner, Breeder, and Trainer Should Know.* Loveland, CO: Alpine Publications, 1999.

——. *The Contented Canine: A Guide to Successful Pet Parenting for Dog Owners.* Lincoln, NE: ASJA Press, 2001.

Case, Linda P. *The Dog: Its Behavior, Nutrition & Health.* Ames, IA: Iowa State University Press/Ames, 1999.

Editors of Prevention Health Books. *Healing with Motion.* Emmaus, PA: Rodale, 1999.

Furman, Sue, Ph.D. *Canine Massage: A Balancing Act.* Wolfchase Press, 2000.

Huber, Stephanie. *Life in the Canine Lane.* Carlsborg, WA: Legacy by Mail, 1999.

Huber, Stephanie and Lesser, Sue Ann, D.V.M. *Physical Therapy for the Canine Athlete.* Johnsville, NY: Flying Dog Press, 1996.

Kidd, Randy, D.V.M., Ph.D. *Dr. Kidd's Guide to Herbal Dog Care.* North Adams, MA: Storey Books, 2000.

Moore, Arden. *50 Simple Ways To Pamper Your Dog.* North Adams, MA: Storey Publishing, 2000.

——. *Dog Training, A Lifelong Guide.* Irvine, CA: BowTie Press, 2002.

——. *Real Food for Dogs.* North Adams, MA: Storey Publishing, 2001.

Moore, Arden and Ackerman, Lowell, D.V.M. *Happy Dog, How Busy People Care for Their Dogs.* Irvine, CA: BowTie Press, 2003.

Palika, Liz. *The New Age Dog.* New York: Renaissance Books, 2001.

——. *All Dogs Need Some Training.* Hoboken, NJ: Wiley, 1997.

Pitcairn, Richard H., D.V.M., Ph.D. and Pitcairn, Susan Hubble. *Dr. Pitcairn's Complete Guide to Natural Health for Dogs & Cats.* Emmaus, PA: Rodale, 1995.

Yeager, Selene. *Selene Yeager's Perfectly Fit.* Emmaus, PA: Rodale, 2001.

Zink, M. Christine, D.V.M., Ph.D. *Dog Health & Nutrition for Dummies.* Hoboken, NJ: Wiley, 2001.

——. *Peak Performance: Coaching the Canine Athlete.* Canine Sports Productions, 1997.

# Appendix D

\* \* \* \* \* \* \* \* \*

# TERMINOLOGY

\* \* \* \* \* \* \* \*

**acupuncture/acupressure:** Both are based on relieving pain and improving the function of organ systems in the body by maintaining a balance of the body's energy life force known as "chi." Acupuncture uses special narrow needles and acupressure uses hand pressure to unblock specific energy flow channels, called meridians, on the body.

**amino acids:** Called the building blocks of protein, the essential and nonessential amino acids total 23. When a dog eats protein, his body breaks down the protein into amino acids that are then absorbed by his body. The 10 essential amino acids for dogs are arginine, isoleucine, histidine, leucine, lysine, methionine, phenylalanine, threonine, tryptophan, and valine.

**antioxidants:** These compounds provide oxidation protection to the cell membranes and DNA from harmful oxygen molecules known as free radicals. Free radicals can damage membranes and trigger heart disease, cancer, arthritis, and other degenerative diseases. Mixed tocopherols are often added to the fats in commercial dog food to prevent rancidity and preserve freshness.

**calorie:** A unit by which energy is measured. Food energy is measured in kilocalories (1000 calories equal 1 kilocalorie). One kilocalorie is the amount of energy needed to heat one gram of water one degree centigrade.

**carbohydrates:** Sugars, starches, and fibers comprise carbohydrates, the body's primary source of energy. There are simple carbohydrates, called sugars, which include honey, white table sugar, and natural sugars found in fruits, vegetables, and milk. There are complex carbohydrates, called starches, which include foods like cooked beans, oatmeal, pasta, potatoes, and rice.

**carnivore:** An animal that eats only meat.

**chondroitin sulfates:** These long chains of sugar molecules act like magnets to attract fluid into the joint's cartilage matrix. Dogs need fluid to move their joints easily.

**dietary fat:** This nutrient provides a good, concentrated source of energy, improves the taste of foods, aids in digestion, and transports fat-soluble vitamins A, D, E, and K throughout the body. Compared to carbohydrates and protein, fats contain about 2.5 times more energy per pound. Essential fatty acids include linoleic, linolenic, and arachdonic acids.

**fiber:** This is a catch-all term for plant tissues found in the seeds, leaves, and stems of plants. Fiber aids the passage of food through the digestive system and helps form firm stools. Dietary fiber also provides a feeling of fullness.

**free radicals:** Highly reactive and destructive molecules made inside the body. They contain one or more unpaired electrons and create chemical imbalances by stealing electrons from healthy molecules. Unchecked, free radicals can cause premature aging and contribute to chronic diseases.

**glucosamine:** Made from an amino acid, called glutamine, and glucose, a body sugar. Glucosamine helps bones, cartilage, skin, hair, and other body tissues.

**glucose:** A monosaccharide, it is better known as blood sugar or dextrose.

**herbal medicine:** The use of plants medicinally has been practiced for thousands of years. Active constituents inside a plant's flowers, petals, stems, and/or roots can be used to prevent or treat a variety of physical and mental conditions. Herbal medicines work with the body's immune system to fight disease and improve the emotional and mental wellbeing of animals.

**herbivore:** An animal that eats only plants.

**immune system:** The body's internal army that identifies and battles foreign invaders, such as viruses and bacterium.

**lactose intolerance:** A condition that results from the inability to digest lactose, a milk sugar; it causes bloating, gas, diarrhea, and other gastrointestinal symptoms.

**metabolism:** The rate by which the body builds up and breaks down the chemicals it needs to live.

**minerals:** These inorganic elements are needed for normal body functions plus bone and tissue development. Major minerals include calcium, phosphorus, potassium, sodium, chloride, magnesium, and sulfur; trace minerals consist of iron, iodine, zinc, chromium, selenium, fluoride, molybdenum, copper, and manganese.

**omnivore:** An animal that eats meat and plants.

**organic:** This term refers to meats, grains, and fruits free of commercial fertilizers or pesticides as well as artificial colors, flavors or preservatives.

**protein:** This essential nutrient comes in animal and plant form and performs many jobs. Protein repairs tissue, provides energy, ensures muscle growth and aids blood, hormones, and the body's immune system. Growing puppies generally require more protein in their diets than older adult dogs. Non-meat sources of protein include soybean meal and tofu.

**vitamins:** Organic, essential nutrients required in small amounts by the body to promote and regulate various physiological processes. Water-soluble vitamins include Vitamin C and the eight B vitamins (thiamin, riboflavin, niacin, $B_6$, $B_{12}$, folate, biotin, and pantothenic acid). Fat-soluble vitamins consist of vitamins A, D, E, and K.